The
Women's Stage Monologues
of 1994

St. Louis Community College
at Meramec
Library

Smith and Kraus *Books For Actors*

THE MONOLOGUE SERIES

The Best Men's / Women's Stage Monologues of 1992
The Best Men's / Women's Stage Monologues of 1991
The Best Men's / Women's Stage Monologues of 1990
One Hundred Men's / Women's Stage Monologues from the 1980's
2 Minutes and Under: Character Monologues for Actors
Street Talk: Character Monologues for Actors
Uptown: Character Monologues for Actors
Monologues from Contemporary Literature: Volume I
Monologues from Classic Plays
100 Great Monologues from the Renaissance Theatre
100 Great Monologues from the Neo-Classical Theatre
100 Great Monologues from the 19th C. Romantic and Realistic Theatres

FESTIVAL MONOLOGUE SERIES

The Great Monologues from the Humana Festival
The Great Monologues from the EST Marathon
The Great Monologues from the Women's Project
The Great Monologues from the Mark Taper Forum

YOUNG ACTORS SERIES

Great Scenes and Monologues for Children
New Plays from A.C.T.'s Young Conservatory
Great Scenes for Young Actors from the Stage
Great Monologues for Young Actors
Multicultural Monologues for Young Actors
Multicultural Scenes for Young Actors

SCENE STUDY SERIES

Scenes From Classic Plays 468 B.C. to 1960 A.D.
The Best Stage Scenes of 1993
The Best Stage Scenes of 1992
The Best Stage Scenes for Men / Women from the 1980's

CONTEMPORARY PLAYWRIGHTS SERIES

Romulus Linney: 17 Short Plays
Eric Overmyer: Collected Plays
Lanford Wilson: 21 Short Plays
William Mastrosimone: Collected Plays
Horton Foote: 4 New Plays
Israel Horovitz: 16 Short Plays
Terrence McNally: 15 Short Plays
Humana Festival '93: The Complete Plays
Humana Festival '94: The Complete Plays
Women Playwrights: The Best Plays of 1992
Women Playwrights: The Best Plays of 1993

GREAT TRANSLATION FOR ACTORS SERIES

The Wood Demon by Anton Chekhov

CAREER DEVELOPMENT SERIES

The Camera Smart Actor
The Sanford Meisner Approach
The Actor's Chekhov
Kiss and Tell: Restoration Scenes, Monologues, & History
Cold Readings: Some Do's and Don'ts for Actors at Auditions

If you require pre-publication information about upcoming Smith and Kraus books, you may receive our semi-annual catalogue, free of charge, by sending your name and address to *Smith and Kraus Catalogue, P.O. Box 127, One Main Street, Lyme, NH 03768. Or call us at (800) 895-4331, fax (603) 795-4427.*

The Best
Women's Stage Monologues
of 1994

edited by Jocelyn A. Beard

The Monologue Audition Series

SK
A Smith and Kraus Book

Published by Smith and Kraus, Inc.
One Main Street, Lyme, NH 03768

Copyright © 1994 by Smith and Kraus, Inc.
All rights reserved
Manufactured in the United States of America

First Edition: November 1994
10 9 8 7 6 5 4 3 2 1

CAUTION: Professionals and amateurs are hereby warned that the plays represented in this book are subject to a royalty. They are fully protected under the copyright laws of the United States of America, and of all countries covered by the International Copyright Union (including the Dominion of Canada and the rest of the British Commonwealth), and of all countries covered by the Pan-American Copyright Convention and the Universal Copyright Convention, and of all countries with which the United States has reciprocal copyright relations. All rights, including professional, amateur, motion picture, recitation, lecturing, public reading, radio broadcasting, television, video or sound taping, all other forms of mechanical or electronic reproductions such as information storage and retrieval systems and photocopying, and the rights of translation into foreign languages, are strictly reserved. Pages 101–106 constitute an extension of this copyright page.

The Monologue Audition Series ISSN 1067-134X

NOTE: These monologues are intended to be used for audition and class study; permission is not required to use the material for those purposes. However, if there is a paid performance of any of the monologues included in this book, please refer to the permissions acknowledgment pages to locate the source who can grant permission for public performance.

Contents

Preface

"Potent" is a word that describes women's roles in theatre in 1994. From the captured Cherokee bride in Robert Schenkkan's THE KENTUCKY CYCLE to the loony new Desdemona in Paula Vogel's DESDEMONA: A PLAY ABOUT A HANDKERCHIEF, the female characters of 1994 are ripe with possibility. In this season we were introduced to a Cambodian women struggling to survive the Killing Fields (THE SURVIVOR: A CAMBODIAN ODYSSEY), a woman battling cancer (MY LEFT BREAST), a white plantation owner giving birth to a mixed-race baby (THE DARKER FACE OF EARTH), and a woman who refuses to help her HIV positive son (BEFORE IT HITS HOME). Mothers, daughters, sisters and lovers; the women of 1994 cover a remarkable expanse of emotional terrain producing many terrific monologues.

You simple can't go wrong with a season that has included work from the likes of Gloria Naylor, Harold Prince, Richard Nelson, Harold Pinter, Terrence McNally, Tony Kushner and Martin Crimp! They're all in here as well as many fresh new voices from here and abroad whose wonderful monologues have been collected for you here in this book. So if you've always wanted to play a TV sitcom writer, a maid of honor, the sister of Sean O'Casey, an angel, a ghost, an abused wife who sells her story to a television producer of a Mexican soap opera diva, then my advice to you is to start reading!

Break a leg!

—*Jocelyn A. Beard*
Patterson, NY
Autumn, 1994

I would like to dedicate this book to A. Katherine Kitowski, friend extraordinaire and the very best Aunt Kathy in the whole wide world.

Introduction

They say that if a director starts day one of rehearsals with a well–chosen cast and a workable groundplan, his or her job is already two–thirds completed. The same can be said of an actor choosing a monologue. If you invest time and care in making your selections, you will have a road map that will sustain and guide you as you make your way.

Your monologues are, in fact, your calling card into the profession. More revealing than the clothes you wear, they announce who you are: your judgement, your capabilities, your level of self-awareness. In choosing and rehearsing them, you must think like a producer ("Is the material fresh and appealing?"), like a director ("How do I shape this scene?") and, of course, like an actor ("How can I get to the root honesty of a moment?"). You carry all the creative responsibilities of a solo performance artist, with one exception—you must filter your own sensibilities through the words of someone else; i.e. the playwright. This is where THE BEST WOMEN'S STAGE MONOLOGUES OF 1994 will prove itself invaluable. The 57 monologues found within this volume provide such a dazzling array of style, theme and character that you are bound to connect with not just one, but several. The editor has kept a remarkably sensitive ear to the ground, offering up a collection of work so far ranging and up-to-the-minute, that it may also serve as a producer's guide to the contemporary American theatre scene as it exists right now.

For example, Paula Vogel stands OTHELLO on its ear with the funny and inventive DESDEMONA, A PLAY ABOUT A HANDKERCHIEF while Theresa Rebeck provides a hip and knowing articulation of the world of sit-coms. And so it goes, the spiritual journey of "Margaret" in Terrence McNally's A PERFECT GANESH is just pages away from the edgy political fantasies of Tony Kushner's SLAVS!. From Eve Ensler to Marion Issac McClinton; Susan Miller to Pearl Cleage, you are treated to a veritable banquet of viewpoints and possibilities.

Just remember, though, that a monologue is not forever. It should fit you like a translucent second skin—expanding as you grow and always revealing the actor within. There will come a time in your evolution that you will seek a new vehicle for expression, and when that happens, Smith and Kraus will surely provide another remarkable anthology like this one to assist you.

In the meanwhile, we "on the other side of the table" eagerly await you and hope your audition will provide us both with insight, surprise and a mutual appreciation of theater's great power.

—*Sara Garonzik*
Producing Artistic Director
Philadelphia Theatre Company

The Best
Women's Stage Monologues
of 1994

Alchemy of Desire/ Dead-Man's Blues
Caridad Svich

Scene: An open, fluid space evocative of a burnt-out bayou, the present
Dramatic
  Simone: a woman mourning the death of her husband, 20-30

Jamie has been killed in an unspecified war. Following his funeral, Simone contemplates the mess left behind by those who had come to the house to pay their respects as well as her love for Jamie.

SIMONE: Chicken.
Buckets and buckets of fried chicken all over.
Twelve, sixteen, twenty-four piece . . .
Everybody brought one. One kind or another.
Caroline, Selah, Mrs. Hawkins . . .
They all came in with their chicken.
They all came in.
With their mouths open. Gristle stuck between their teeth.
Their faces smeared with grease, and perfume, and liquor.
They all came in.
Came in and flapped their arms. Callin' out to God
and Jeremiah and all the powers in the universe.
They all came in with their chicken.
Came in to push their thigh-meat in my face.
Push it in my face to make me feel better.

I thought I'd puke.
I thought, "One more bucket, I'm gona get down on my knees
and puke right next to the coffin."

I don't like fried chicken. He sure as hell didn't.
Why'd they bring it then? 'Cause that's what you do?

That's what you do when someone passes on?
Y'know, just because people been doin' somethin' a long time
don't mean you gotta KEEP on doin' it.
Ain't nobody said you gotta become a fool to tradition.
Why didn't they bring somethin' else?
Sweet potato pie, ice water, hard whiskey . . .
I wouldn't 've minded some hard whiskey.
But fried chicken?

It smells up the whole house.
Smells up the house real good.
Why, you can smell the stink of the fat for miles.
. . .

Clear up to the river, you can smell it.

Grease all over.
Goes straight through the buckets, stains the wood.
HELL to get grease out once it's stained the wood.
Fingers get oily, sticky. Hands reekin' of chicken.
Grease swimmin' through you til NOTHIN'
can rid you of its reek.
Gotta get tar soap, wash it off, scrub your hands blood raw
to get rid of it.

And the thing is, who's gonna eat it?
Who is gonna eat the damn chicken anyway?
I can't eat it.– And he's dead.
What good's it gonna do him?
. . .

Peel off the skin and fat and throw the chicken bones at him,
that's all I can do.
Bury him with the chicken bones.

Dead.
He's just dead.

Some bullet ripped right through him like he was dog-meat:
eyes all busted, bones stickin' out of the flesh . . .
I didn't even recognize him.
If they didn't say it was Jamie, I wouldn't know
who it was, so little left of him that's really him.

(*Sound: slightly distorted shell-fire in battle. Fade.*)

He was my husband, Jamie was.
Damn war killed him off.
I don't even know where it was.
All I know is: one day, there was a rumor of war
and the next, he was off to some little country
somewhere I couldn't even find on a map.
and then he was dead.
    . . .

We weren't even married a month.
Made love in some car, got married . . .
And he just TAKES OFF.

BASTARD.
    . . .

(*Sound: slightly distorted shell-fire. Fade.*)

I can barely remember him now.
I'll see somebody, he'll look like him,
but he'll turn 'round and I realize
he don't look like Jamie at all.

Not even married a month.
And all I got are buckets of chicken
stinkin' up the house. That's all I got.
Fried chicken and a dead body.
(*Lights fade.*)

Alchemy of Desire/ Dead-Man's Blues

Caridad Svich

Scene: An open, fluid space evocative of a burnt-out bayou, the present
Dramatic
> Simone: a woman mourning the death of her husband, 20-30

> *Simone has been driven to the edge by haunting visitations from Jamie. Here, she burns his clothes in an effort to break from the past.*

SIMONE: You got to burn things.
Gotta burn 'em so they'll go away.
You don't burn 'em, they just stick around forever.
You burn things, they go away.

They disappear down the path of nothin'-ness
where fire and ash and air get all mixed up together
and turn into sky and breathin'.

That's what they tell me, anyway.

'Cept the more I burn things,
the more they stay in my mind.:

the blue shirt
he wore when we were out by the water,
the way he looked at me then, and took his hand
and ran it along inside me,
so a trickle of sweat stayed, restin', on his brow
wonderin' where it was gonna go next;

(*Throws shirt into fire.*) YOU BURN THINGS, THEY GO AWAY.

the shape of his torso
permanently outlined
in the small folds and crisp creases
of his grease-stained work-shirt
fresh with the smell of gasoline, and oil and . . .
all the other mysteries of the garage;

(*Throws shirt into fire.*) YOU BURN 'EM, THEY GO AWAY.

the softness of his skin
in the white jersey
comin' up behind me in the kitchen
while I was cookin' the chicken fricassee,
'n the steam was comin' up out of the pot
and he was squeezin' me firm, soft in his white jersey —
jersey he wore with no underpants on,
so that the sweat and smell of his member
became part of that jersey
as much as its frayed cotton fibers and green number 2-1;

(*Throws jersey into the fire.*)

Things have a way of stayin' in the mind.

No burnin' can stop your mind from thinkin'.
Only by losin' yourself completely
can you stop yourself from thinkin'.
Either that, or by dyin'.

Nobody knows for sure whether you keep thinkin'
once you're dead, but I figure once you're gone
from this world, the things of this world
can't be the same.
And that's GOT to be comfortin' somehow.
To NOT THINK.

  . . .

(*To self.*) burn things. go away.
  . . .

It's takin' myself down that's hard.
Every time I try –
lettin' the spark brush 'gainst my skin
holdin' my breath
'til I feel myself drown in the gulf of fire –
the too-much-ness of this life
calls to me
and brings me back
from

Ash.
They're all of a piece now:
blue, white, sweat, smells –
locked in flame.

(*To self.*) burn things. don't go away.

The Autobiography of
Aiken Fiction
Kate Moira Ryan

Scene: Here and now
Serio-Comic
    Jos Lubenowich, a high school senior, 17

While playing a game of Trivial Pursuit with her friend, Jos relates the story of her meeting with Tallulah Bankhead.

O   O   O

Jos: Mother was always on the road. She played everyone from the Duchess of Malfi to Ma Rose to Miss Hannigan.

[Aiken: Man, I wish my Mom was an actress instead of a product tester.]

Jos: Oh, I come from a long line of grease paint craving egomaniacs. The Lubenowich's were like the Barrymores of Poland. The only difference was that we performed in Yiddish. We continued the tradition upon our emigration to the US of A. So when *The Milktrain* was on Broadway, I was taken to see the divine Miss Bankhead. Having only Romper Room and Sesame Street as my point of reference, I loved it. She ranked right up there with Mr. Greenjeans. After the show we went backstage and there she was in her silk kimono with that insane tousled hair. She looked straight at me and screamed, "Get that midget out of here!" I burst into a wide grin and fainted for I knew this was a force more powerful than Santa Claus and the Easter Bunny combined. When I awoke, I was laying on her chaise lounge being gently fanned. This voice laced with whiskey asked, "Kid, you think you're well enough to go to Sardis with your Mum and I?" I nodded. "Yes, yes take me to Sardis." That evening I slurped my milk loudly, grateful for the annoyed expression on Miss Bankhead's face. As she tore the glass away from me, I saw driblets of milkiness drip down my straw and I thought to myself, 'this is living.' Then I fell asleep and when I awoke in my hand was a piece of kimono. Tattered red silk with a calla lily print.

Bailey's Cafe

Gloria Naylor

Scene: A narrow street that clings to the end of the world on a barren strip of earth.
  World Time: 1948
Dramatic
    Jesse Bell: one tough cookie with a soft center, 40s

Here, Jesse reveals her life's tragedy as well as her love affair with heroin.

O O O

JESSE: I'm gonna tell you why people get high. 'Cause when you're that far up there, everything becomes clear. I ain't lying, crystal clear. I mean, you can see *everything* about your life, all at one time. 'Cause you high, ya know, way up high. So you sniff the horse. Then you pop the horse. And after a while the only decent ride is through the mainline. I'm not making no excuses for becoming a junkie. In fact, I was glad I discovered heroin. Yeah, I was glad – do you hear me? – glad. 'Cause when that dyke club got raided and Uncle Eli used every bit of influence he had to make sure my name hit the newspapers and stayed in the papers, throwing dirt on everything about my life, just digging, digging, until they dug up my special friend and my husband had to say, *had* to say, he didn't know 'cause, after all, he was a man and a King and there was his son to consider, so I'm out there by myself, on display like a painted dummy in a window as the name Jesse Bell came to mean that no-good slut from the docks and the nineteen years I'd put into my marriage didn't amount to dog shit, the care I'd given my son – dog shit – the clothes I wore, the music I liked, the school I went to, the family I came from, everything that made me, *me* – dog shit, 'cause nobody was interested in my side of the story, not the reporters, not the neighbors, not the divorce court, nobody, 'cause everybody was standing around like vultures looking at me fall fall fall, waiting for me to smash my brains on the pavement, yeah, waiting for me to lose my mind;

and within an inch of the ground, within an inch of having my head split open and my brains spill out, Jesse Bell grabbed onto the reins of that white horse, letting 'em all see her spread wings as she rose . . . She rose . . . She rose . . . (*A beat*) I will cry no more!

Before It Hits Home
Cheryl L. West

Scene: Here and now
Dramatic
    Reba: a woman who has just discovered that her son is dying of AIDS, 50s

When Wendal comes home to fight his illness, Reba cannot accept him. She can't even bring herself to touch the things that he has touched. Here, Reba blames Wendal for the death of everything she ever loved.

○   ○   ○

REBA: Shut up. Just shut up. Don't say a word. I heard enough from you last night to last me a lifetime. I'm about to walk out that door and try and explain to that man out there why I don't have a home no more. I hate what you've done to my house, Wendal. Spent my life here, inside these walls, trying to stay safe, keep my family safe . . . didn't know any better, maybe if I had, I could deal with what you done brought in here. See this slipcover, I made it. And that afghan, I made that too, these curtains . . . I made this tablecloth, see this lace. I made you. My son! And I took such pride . . . but last night you made me realize I hadn't made nothing, not a damn thing . . . been walking around fooling myself . . . It's hard to look at something . . . I mean I look around here and it's like somebody came in and smeared shit all over my walls . . . I'm scared to touch anything . . . you hear me, Wendal, scared to touch anything in my own house . . . Nothing. Maybe if I could get outside these walls I could . . . I can't stay here and watch it fester, crumble down around me . . . right now I can't help you . . . I can hardly stand to even look at you . . . I can't help your father . . . what good am I? I don't know anymore. I just know this house is closing in on me and I got to get out of here.

Body Politic
Steve Murray

Scene: A classroom
Serio-Comic
    Kath: an actress-turned-acting teacher, 30s

  Here, Kath conducts an interesting class discussion on "The Tempest."

O   O   O

KATH: Now. "The Tempest." You can look at this play as an allegory for Shakespeare's art, Prospero standing in for the playwright, looking back over a fruitful life. The enchanted island, the geography of Shakespeare's complete work – how many plays, Tony? . . . Right, 36. Like Shakespeare, Prospero is a stage manager, he's the writer and the director both, rattling the thunder sheet, deploying all the stage actors. He's a puppeteer, the other characters, pawns of his agenda. Miranda, for instance. Stupid young Miranda. Think a teenage Vanna White. This girl whose purpose it is to deliver the dumb blond joke. Here she is, facing this crew of drunken sailors, corrupt nobles, would-be murderers, *her* murderer: "Oh Brave New World that has such people in't." As an actress, when I acted, when I still acted regularly, I always had a problem with this play. The idiot girl, controlled by these men. Yes? Yes, Linda, good point, she doesn't know any better, *she* has an excuse. So, everyone hops into the boat and sails away, happy ending. This is what art does. Life isn't so simple, you can't plot it out. Though we pretend. We play assigned roles to give us a sense of order. And so long as we conform to society's script – the loving wife, the sensitive man. Play your part, you're ok. If not, violence. Sorry, listen to me, I'm teaching civics. Miranda, she's so gullible. Caliban forces himself on her, she can't see him for what he is, a monster. Shakespeare makes the world of "The Tempest" black-and-white. He splits in two this mutant blend of angel and demon we all carry around inside us. Now in real life, Ariel might look like an angel, but he could be the rapist. This is what art does: Takes the sprawling raw material of the world and shapes it into narrative coherence. Well, art and soap operas. Shakespeare sits in his sandbox, pushing toy monsters and lovers and murderers around till it looks like they're dancing. In the real world, you never know who you'll meet on the island.

Careless Love
Len Jenkin

Scene: Here and now
Serio-Comic
    Marlene: a middle-aged lounge singer, 40-50

Here, a road-weary lounge singer raps with the audience.

O   O   O

MARLENE: Thank you. Thank you all so much.

You know, love is a Mystery. Capital M. It's a cracked window in a strange hotel room, look out down the alley to a violet streetlamp on the boulevard, down the boulevard to the city line, climb halfway up a ragged hillside over the highway, get your back against a tree and wait. Light up a smoke and wait for something. Love is in that waiting, little blue glow on the earth line tells you it's day and the night has ended.

You're in the kitchen and the butter goes sizzle in the pan, and you pour in two eggs, and stir 'em around, look over your shoulder and she got the little bunny's head in her orange juice and she's laughing and laughing.

Somebody just opens their blue eyes wide, and lets you look inside.

Now is the hour of the dragon, that hour of the deep night when our hearts are open. Sharing is caring. And total sharing is total caring. We care about every one of you. We wish you peace.

Have a last one – 'cause it's just about closing time. And when you get home tonight, safe in bed – right before you drift off to sleep, take a moment, and think on Spin and me.

(*A long silence.*)

You'll be back here tomorrow night. I know you will. I asked the bartender to put a little "comeback" in your drink . . .

The Cavalcaders
Billy Roche

Scene: Ireland
Dramatic
　　Nuala: an emotionally unstable young woman in love with an older man, 20s

Following a passionate lovemaking session, Nuala tells Terry, her lover, about a poem that she's working on.

O　　　　O　　　　O

NUALA: The Pelican is the noblest bird of them all, yeh know. She sacrifices herself for her young. Yeh see when her children are born and begin to grow up they flap about and beat their wings and that and they hit the mother and father in the face all the time until one of them becomes angry and strikes them back and accidently kills them. After that the mother sort of mourns for a few days and then on the third day she'll pierce her breast and open her side and she'll lay across her little babes, pouring out her blood all over the dead bodies and this brings them back to life again. That's what my poem is all about, yeh see. The Noble Pelican! . . . River Reddens. Swan Serene. Wonders As She Wanders Through The Dead Of Night. Blood Soaked Morning Stains The Day. As Two Dead Babes Come Out To Play . . . But sure there's another one in there about the Rowan Tree. The Rowan Tree is supposed to possess some sort of mystical powers, yeh know, to ward off evil spirits or somethin'. When I was young we used to have one growin' up around the house. Its branches touched my little bedroom window. Made me feel really safe – like I was sleepin' in the arms of a big gentle giant or somethin'. Our house used to look out on an auld spooky graveyard like, yeh know? Are yeh alright?

Connie and Sabrina In Waiting

Sandra Marie Vargo

Scene: A funeral parlour
Serio-Comic
    Sabrina: a woman attending her best friend's funeral, 50s

Sabrina's best friend, Connie, has died of a heart attack. Here, Sabrina shares a last moment together with the coffin.

    ○   ○   ○

SABRINA: Could use a scotch, though. Don't suppose there's a bar in this joint . . . Hell've a way to hear about this, Con . . . a message on my machine. (*She goes to the coffin.*) So much for promises. You gave me your solemn word this time. "No way I'm missin' this dinner date, 'Brina," that's what you said. "It's been twenty-five years since we ate spaghetti and drank Blue Nun at Jimmy B's. I'm just dyin' to see if Stanley still has any of that beautiful curly hair!" . . . Sure, just dyin' . . . I meant it, Con, when I said I wouldn't stand for any more phoney excuses. Standin' me up again! (*Pause.*) Connie Ann Louisa Maria . . . (*She chuckles to herself at the pet name.*) Dyin' to find out about Stanley's hair, huh? Couldn't wait to have a plate of spaghetti, huh? You have any idea how long I waited at that bar?! You know how many glasses of Blue Nun I hadda drink? . . . Oh, and the spaghetti, I not only ate both plates, with meatballs, but I forced down two orders of cheese garlic bread . . . just for you! Just 'cause I knew you'd order it for us . . . I don't even like cheese garlic bread! (*Pause.*) He's losin' most of it . . . Stanley. Everybody was sorry they missed you. Binky played that damned "Volare" a hunnerd and fifty-seven times and Jimmy B played "That's Amore," just for you. You shoulda been there. The whole place chimed in on, "when the moon hit'sa your eye like a bigga pizza pie" . . . even me. (*She laughs.*) Okay, I know, so I can't sing. So we all got our own kinda hell . . . Oops, sorry. I mean not that I think for one minute that

that's where a very old but unreliable friend of mine mighta made a pit stop, but it's not a word I should use loosely, under the circumstances. After all, we were never what could've been even remotely misconstrued as angelic material. (*Pause.*) You were, after all, always getting me into trouble.

The Darker Face of the Earth

Rita Dove

Scene: A plantation in ante-bellum South Carolina
Dramatic
   Amalia: owner of the plantation who has just given birth to a mixed-race baby, 20s

When her husband sees that the baby is clearly half black, he threatens to find the slave who has "offended" Amalia and have him whipped to death. Here, Amalia corrects his assumption of rape.

О   О   О

AMALIA: It wasn't rape, and you know it.
He brought iced lemon water
up to my room and left
half an hour later.
Everyday you saw him –
but did you ever say one word?
(*To the Doctor.*)
Daddy knew he was weak.
He tried to keep me from
marrying him, but I was in love
with riding boots and the smell
of shaving cream and bourbon.
I was in love with a cavalry man
and nothing could stop me,
not even Daddy!
But not even daddy suspected
where you would seek your satisfaction.
As long as you let a slave man
bring your wife iced drinks
instead of doing it yourself,
as long as a black man crawled over
the perfumed limbs of your wife,
and you thought you had all
the freedom in the world –

18

it was your right
to pull on those riding boots
and stalk little slave girls.
You enjoy their fear,
don't you? God knows
what you do to them in
the name of ownership.
And now, dear Louis,
in the name of ownership
you will not harm this child
or the father of this child.

Desdemona
a play about a handkerchief
Paula Vogel

Scene: The Palace on Cyrpus, ages ago
Serio-Comic
    Bianca: a whore, 20s

Bianca has been recrafted as a lusty prostitute in this retellng of Othello. Here, she entertains Desdemona and Emilia with a tale of one of her quirkier johns.

○　　○　　○

BIANCA: Well, there's this one john, an owld mate, who's been on tick for some weeks, an' 'e's got quite a bill. But Aw feels sorry for 'im' 'is wife really lams 'im at 'ome, an' Aw figures 'e need t' get it off 'is chest – So 'e comes in, an' Aw says: "Tom – you owe me over two quid, now; when's it comin'?" "Gaw, Bianca," 'e says, "Aw just been out o' Collar, an' – "
[DESDEMONA: – "Out of Collar?"]
BIANCA: Wot yew call un-deployed . . .
"Bianca," 'e says, "Gawd luv yew, me owld woman an' Aw've had a row an' Aw'm all done in. Aw'll pay th' soddin' bill, some'ow; but fer now, fer owld times," 'e says – well Gawd's Wounds, wot was Aw t'do? "Right, then, Tom," Aw said, an' Aw lays down on the bed – 'cause 'e liked me to go first – an' 'e puts the straps on me – "Tom," Aw says, "listen, luv, th' straps are bleedin' tight – " An' before Aw knew wot, 'e was lammin' me for real!! 'E did me fer a jacketin' such as Aw thought would be me last L 'n' B!! Aw bite me teeth not to scream, 'cause the bobbies won't put up with no row, no matter how many quid Aw pay 'em . . . Well, Tom finally gets it over wif, an' it's *my* turn. "Aw'm sorry, Bianca," 'e says, "if Aw got a bit rough." "Oh, it's nofin', Tom," Aw says – 'cause Aw'm determined t' get me own back . . . So Aw tie 'im down on th' bed – 'e's a big strapper o' a bloke – An' then; Aw lam th' *pudding* out o' 'im – !! An' 'e's 'ollerin' like

it's th' Second Coming. Then after Aw gi' 'im a royal pasting, Aw go through 'is togs, an' in the back pocket – Aw find a soddin' crown! "You been 'olding out on me, Tom! Aw've had it wi' yer dodges an' flams – wot kind o' a soup kitchen do yew fink me?" – An' Aw let into 'im again!! – "Bianca – let me go, an' Aw'll niver flam to ye again!" "BLEEDIN'-RIGHT!" Aw says. So Aw copped 'is brass, takes up the belt, an' let 'im loose – straight into the street 'e runs, naked as a blue-jay – Aw had to throw 'is togs after 'im. "Yew Owld Stringer!" Aw yelled: – "'Ere's yer togs, an' fer yer change, take this!" (*Bianca raises her fist and slaps her elbow; excited, she catches her breath.*)

Desdemona
a play about a handkerchief
Paula Vogel

Scene: The Palace on Cyprus, ages ago
Dramatic
    Emilia: wife of Iago and maid to Desdemona, 30s

When Desdemona discovers that Cassio has given her handkerchief to Bianca, she knows that she's in big trouble with Othello. She pleads her case to Emilia, not knowing that it was she who took the handkerchief in the first place. The two share several glasses of wine, and Emilia reveals the following insight into the relationship between married people.

EMILIA: When I was married in the Church, the knot tied beneath the Virgin's nose, I looked forward to the bed with as much joy as any girl after a hard day. And then Iago – well, he was still a lad, with the softness of a boy, and who could tell he'd turn into the man? (*Emilia pauses to drink.*) But all that girl-nonsense was knocked out of me by the nights. Night followin' night, as sure as the day's work came after. I'd stretch myself out on the bed, you see, waitin' for my good man to come to me and be my mate – as the Priest said he could – but then. But then I saw it didn't matter what had gone on between us – the fights, my crying, a good meal or a cold one. Days could pass without a word between us – and he'd take his fill of me the same. I could have been the bed itself. And so, you see, I vowed not to be there for him. As he'd be lying on me in the dark, I'd picture up my rosary, so real I could kiss the silver. And I'd start at the Blessed Cross itself, while he was somewhere doin' his business above, and I'd say the first wooden bead, and then I'd finger the next bead in my mind, and then onto the next – (*Emilia stops.*) But I never did make it to the medallion. He'd be all through with me by the time of the third "Hail Mary." (*Pause.*) Does my lady know what I'm saying?
[DESDEMONA: I'm not sure. I . . . I don't think it's . . . happened to

me like that.]

EMILIA: Ah, well, men are making fools of themselves over you. The Ambassador is traipsing from the mainland just to hold onto your skirt; and your husband – (*Emilia stops herself.*) – Well, maybe it's all different for the likes of you. (*Desdemona says nothing.*) And then, maybe not. It's hard to be seeing, when you're young and men watch you when you pass them by, and the talkin' stops between them. But all in all, in time you'll know. Women just don't figure in their heads – not the one who hangs the wash, not Bianca – and not even you, m'lady. That's the hard truth. Men only see each other in their eyes. Only each other.

The Ends of the Earth
Morris Panych

Scene: Here and now
Serio-Comic
>   Willy: a woman with conceptual problems, any age.

Willy is an unusual woman who seems to be the proprietess of a ramshackle hotel on an island at the end of the world. Willy doesn't seem to experience the same reality as the other characters in the play, and here tells two of her guests how she happened to arrive at the hotel so many years ago.

○   ○   ○

WILLY: (*Suddenly, after a long pause, lightning.*) Oh. I forgot I was here. (*Pause.*) Well, would you care for anything now that I am? (*Pause.*) I don't mind Mr. Travers. I like to be of some use around here, since nobody else is. It's been like this for as long as I can remember. I arrived here, once, just like everybody else. There wasn't so much as a bellman to collect my things. I went to my room and just sat on my bed. For days. Alice would drift by in a dream, now and again, and disappear. "What a strange way she has of running things" I thought. Not a towel or a tea biscuit to be had. Days passed into weeks and I began to really wonder. I had to make my own breakfast, my own bed. One day, passing by Alice's room, and noticing she wasn't anywhere about, I snuck in and peeked around. But – no sooner had I entered when she came charging up from behind me. "Well!" she said, "It's about time you made up the room. The service in this place is terrible!!" She thought I was the management, you see, and I found myself surrendering to her conviction. Over time. But don't tell Alice. She'd be very upset. You know how she is with guests. And she'd hardly be pleased to discover I was one. After all this time. Who wants to know that there's no one in charge of things? It leaves us with nobody to complain about. When things go wrong. As they so often do. But one does wonder when on earth they're going to finally show up, these absentee proprietors. I'm staying only as long as that. To pay my bill. And I'll be on my way once again. In the meantime, you must forgive poor Alice. She doesn't see things the way you and I do. As a matter of fact, she doesn't see them at all. So quite naturally she assumes that you're evil. People are always much worse when you imagine them.

The Family of Mann
Theresa Rebeck

Scene: LA
Serio-Comic
    Clara: a PA working on a sit-com, 20-30

In her lowly capacity of production assistant, Clara has seen it all. Here, she offers her impression of Los Angeles to one of the show's new writers.

○   ○   ○

CLARA: I shouldn't care, you know? I shouldn't even be out here. This town is bad. The first week I'm here, I'm walking around these gorgeous neighborhoods, Santa Monica, Beverly Hills, thinking, where the fuck are the black people? I drove through Compton just for the fuck of it, and that scared me so bad I went back to Beverly Hills. I called my dad in Dallas, he pulled some strings and got me a job on the lot, so then I'm walking around this major fucking studio, thinking, oh man, I work in the big house now. Fucking Bill says sit on my lap, I almost said Yassir, Massa. You walk around the lot, maybe catch a glimpse of Whoopi or Denzel off in the distance, they're like fucking gods, you know, we aren't even on the same planet. And everybody keeps telling me how lucky I am. All my friends? I get paid three hundred bucks a week to run errands for white people, and I'm a lucky girl because I got a *job* on the fucking *lot*. I saw an angel on a street corner, and I didn't even think twice. Wings and shit. The whole nine yards. I didn't even blink. She said, get out now, girl, the day of judgment is at hand, get the fuck out of LA, and I said, what, are you kidding? I got a job on the lot!
(*Pause.*)
[BELINDA: You saw an angel?]
CLARA: Oh fuck, they're everywhere now, you see them all over, what's the big deal? They're in catalogues, for God's sake. Notecards and shit. There was some Broadway play about angels,

they're making a mini-series of it over on the other side of the lot. The place is crawling with angels. Six hundred extras with wings; the whole soundstage looks like this huge, stressed out birdbath. I don't know. The whole thing, it'll kill you if you think about it too hard. Oh, who cares, right? Some of them are real. They have to be. Don't they?

The Family of Mann
Theresa Rebeck

Scene: LA
Serio-Comic
   Clara: a PA working on a sit-com, 20-30

Clara is slowly turning into an angel. As such, she here delivers her opinion on the USA.

     O   O   O

CLARA: This is the way the universe works: Everything moves from imagination to reality. Such is the force of creation. As soon as anyone imagines anything, it is only instants away from becoming real. Magic is the power that makes this happen. Science also has power, but in a smaller way. You think of objects – a telephone, a refrigerator, an airplane, and then, they exist. From the imagination, to the real.

In America, somehow this process has been reversed. Americans look at something that is only imaginary, and then transform the real into that imagined thing. Little girls look at billboards of impossible women and say, that is what I want to be. People watch moving images of beings who could never exist, and say, that is what we are. The real yearns to be imaginary. And so, America is evaporating. This problem is particularly acute in Los Angeles, a city which is, frankly, about to lift off. Maybe that is why they call it the City of the Angels. Although that too is something of a misnomer. Really, we don't like it here.

Five Women Wearing the Same Dress
Alan Ball

Scene: A wedding reception in Knoxville, TN
Serio-Comic
> Georgeanne: a woman carrying a torch for an old flame, 30s

When Georgeanne sees the man with whom she had a flaming affair in college at a friend's wedding she is bombarded with memories – most of them unpleasant.

O   O   O

GEORGEANNE: I was walking down the aisle, first thing I saw was the back of his head. It just jumped right out at me. I recognized that little hair pattern on the back of his neck, where his hair starts? You know where it comes to those two little points, and it's darker than the rest? I always thought that was so sexy. Then I looked at him during the ceremony, and something about the way the light hit his face . . . I swear, it just broke my heart. And then outside, I saw him talking to this total bitch in a navy blue linen dress with absolutely no back, I mean you could almost see her butt. And he was smiling at her with that smile, that same smile that used to make me feel like I really meant something to him. And then it all came back, just bang, all those times I sat waiting for his phone call, me going out of my way to make things convenient for him. Having to take a fucking taxi cab to the Women's Health Center that day because it was so cold my car wouldn't start. And later that awful, awful night I sat out in front of his apartment building staring at Tracy's burgundy Cutlass in the driveway, just wishing I was dead. You know, I started smoking cigarettes that night. And if I ever die of cancer I swear it's going to be Tommy Valentine's fault. (*She lights a cigarette, stands and wanders around listlessly.*) God! I feel like I am going crazy! My cousin George, he's a nurse, he says I am the perfect type to get some weird disease because I'm so emotional.

Five Women Wearing the Same Dress
Alan Ball

Scene: A wedding reception in Knoxville, TN
Serio-Comic
> Mindy: a woman attending her brother's wedding, 30s

Mindy is a lesbian whose lover has been specifically uninvited to her brother's wedding. This, when combined with the usual wedding catastrophes and a good amount of booze, leads Mindy to the following melancholy observations.

O   O   O

MINDY: I knew this day was doomed, from the moment when Scott first told me he was going to marry Tracy. (*Mockingly.*) *Tracy,* who requested that I not bring Deb who is my lover of *nine years* to the rehearsal dinner because they wanted to keep it just *family.* And I acquiesced because I didn't want another big scene, and now Deb is boycotting the wedding which *Tracy* has gone out of her way to let me know she is *very hurt* by. Bitch. (*Pause.*) She will never love my little brother the way he deserves to be loved. She will never *honor* him and *cherish* him, like she said she would today, in front of God and everybody. It just makes me so sad. And now here I am in this ridiculous dress, with a fucking pin cushion on my head, I look like a hooker from the Twilight Zone, and if I blow chunks, I'm going to be really upset. (*Georgeanne has entered during this tirade.*) I hate throwing up. You are totally alone when you throw up.

Floating Rhoda and the Glue Man

Eve Ensler

Scene: Here and now
Serio-Comic
  Rhoda: a woman searching for love and healing, 30s

Rhoda is someone who has been hurt by life. Here, she tries to recall the time before the pain.

○   ○   ○

RHODA: Before all this, before the bright white electrical hospital lights shining in my just born face, before the fear in my mother's body, before this emptiness and hunger, before this despair, before I confused the past with the present, before everything was the opposite of what it seemed to be, before transference, before I left my body, before the accumulation of things and a desperation for fame and approval, before cocaine, before gin and tonics, before my father broke my hole and my brother woke me by putting alcohol in my eyes, before I learned not to tell the truth, before I became afraid of giving too much or showing the depth of my attachments, before I had braces, before I obsessed about my flat chest, before I picked my face, before I panicked on exams, before losing made me weep violently, before I became revolted by trees and moved to the city, before babies terrorized me and made me want to hurt them, before fax, before I hated cops, before I expected betrayal, before I split into a person inside a person (*Rhoda and Rhoda's stand-in exchange a glance.*) inside a person outside a person inside her, before then, there was light, big light, complete light and I was of the light and in the light and there were wings involved and home.

Flyin' West
Pearl Cleage

Scene: Outside the all-black town of Nicodemus, Kansas, 1898
Dramatic
    MISS LEAH: a black woman born into slavery now living as a free citizen in Nicodemus, 73

Miss Leah has lived more life than most women her age, and accumulated more heartache than many. Here, she describes her first meeting with James, the man she loved, when they were both being used as breeding stock on a southern plantation.

O   O   O

MISS LEAH: There's a lot worse places than this to have a baby. I'd of given anything to a had my babies in my own little house on my own piece of land with James pacing outside and the midwife knowin' what to do to ease you through it. Is that too tight?
[MINNIE: It's perfect!]
[(*Frank gets up and begins dressing in the bedroom. He is wearing more expensive city clothes. He takes great care with his cuff links, tie, etc. He is especially pleased with his hair.*)]
MISS LEAH: (*Resumes her braiding.*) I was only thirteen when I got my first one. They wanted me to start early 'cause I was big and strong. Soon as my womanhood came on me, they took me out in the barn and put James on me. He was older than me and big. He already had children by half the women on the place. Sometimes Colonel Harrison would line all those children up behind him to show some other white man what a good breeder he was. My James . . . (*A beat.*) But that first time, he was hurting me so bad and I was screamin' and carryin' on somethin' awful and that old overseer just watchin' and laughin' to make sure James really doin' it. He watch us every night for a week and after the third one I hear James tryin' to whisper somethin' to me real quiet while he doin' it. I was so surprised I stopped cryin' for a minute and I hear James sayin' "Leah, Leah, Leah . . . " He just kept sayin' my name over and over. (*A beat.*) At the end of the week, I had got my first son.

Flyin' West
Pearl Cleage

Scene: Outside the all-black town of Nicodemus, Kansas, 1898
Dramatic
Miss Leah: a black woman born into slavery now living as a free citizen in Nicodemus, 73

Here, Miss Leah describes the horror of having her babies taken from her at birth and sold to neighboring plantations. She goes on to describe a bit of her life with James following the Civil War and of her need to go west.

MISS LEAH: When they sold my first baby boy offa the place, I felt like I couldn't breath for three days. After that, I could breath a little better, but my breasts were so full of milk they'd soak the front of my dress. Overseer kept telling me he was gonna have to see if nigger milk was really chocolate like they said it was, so I had to stay away from him til my milk stopped runnin'. And one day I saw James and I told him they had sold the baby, but he already knew it. He had twenty been sold offa our place by that time. Never saw any of 'em.

When he told me that, I decided he was gonna at least lay eyes on at least one of his babies came through me. So next time they put us together, I told him that I was gonna be sure this time he got to see his child before Colonel Harrison sold it. But I couldn't. Not that one or the one after or the one after the ones after that. James never saw their faces. Until we got free. Then he couldn't look at 'em long enough. That was a man who loved his children. Hug 'em and kiss 'em and take 'em everywhere he go.

I think when he saw the fever take all five of them, one by one like that . . . racin' each other to heaven . . . it just broke him down. He'd waited so long to have his sons and now he was losing them all again. He was like a crazy man just before he died. So I buried him next to his children and I closed the door on that little piece of house we had and I started walkin' west. If I'd had wings, I'd a set out flyin' west. I needed to be some place big enough for all my sons and all my ghost grandbabies to roam around. Big enough for me to think about all the sweetness they had stole from me and James and just holler about it as loud as I want to holler.

Grace
Doug Lucie

Scene: England, the present
Dramatic
    Ruth: an artistic English gentlewoman, 50s

Ruth's early years were spent in Africa with her missionary parents. Their mission a failure, the family returns to England, where Ruth's sister, Grace, falls victim to a mysterious fatal illness. Grace's death becomes the subject of a book written by their mother in which she details the event with divine visitations. Years later, an American evangelist who is a devotee of Grace's story makes an offer on Ruth's house with the intention of making it the vanguard of his European mission. Driven by her contempt for evangelism, Ruth is forced to finally reveal the truth about Grace's death.

        O   O   O

RUTH: A few words . . . (*Beat.*) Yes. You're right, Freddy. I ask you to forgive me. (*Beat.*) In all the Christian vocabulary, the word which means most to me is probably the simplest, yet the most problematical. It is a word which, whenever I hear it, chimes in my heart with a force I imagine the scriptures do in yours. That word is truth. (*Beat.*) I don't pretend to know any one big truth, I leave that to the men of God. But I have always believed that the truth protects us from pain. Without the truth, we will believe anything. When we believe anything, we become victims of the cruel and the greedy. (*Beat.*) I said I don't know any one big truth. That's not strictly, er, true. The truth is: I have lied to you. And now, I just want to tell the truth. (*Beat.*) I have written a book, an autobiography. I have told the story of my family, and of my sister Grace in particular. Perhaps it would have been more honest of me to have told you this earlier, but I'm afraid I lacked the courage. Or perhaps I was just being greedy. Well. (*Beat.*) The book my mother wrote is pure fantasy from beginning to end. To begin with, our time in Africa was a miserable failure. We bribed many, we converted few. And thanks to my father's only slight grasp of matters scientific, his pioneering irrigation techniques led to many, many deaths. We didn't arrive back in England our work done, we were ordered back in disgrace. Luckily, my grandfather had a better grasp of reality than my father, and he left us Hartstone to come back to. Otherwise we would probably have starved. What an irony that would have been. (*Beat.*) My mother . . . my mother was a devoted Christian, who liked to think she had dedicated her life to God. In actual fact, she dedicated her life to a series of fantasies. She fantasized my father's greatness, she fantasized their achievements in Africa, and, most of all, she fantasized my sister's death. (*Beat.*) Grace was not in the grip of a terminal illness when we returned from Africa. When we returned, she was, in fact, six months, or thereabouts, pregnant. (*Beat.*) It was too late by the time my parents found out to do anything about the baby. And believe me, they would have. Anything rather than live with the truth. Instead, we came back here, and Grace was confined, a prisoner in that tiny room upstairs. From the day we returned, my father never spoke to Grace. As far as I know, he never saw her again. (*Beat.*) She died giving birth. There was no doctor, my mother didn't believe in doctors. I think they hoped the baby would die too, but he was strong, very strong. But poor Grace died in more agony than you will ever be able to imagine. A frightened, tortured fifteen year old girl, left in unbearable pain for hours, to die. (*Beat.*) I like to think that Christ would have appeared and gently led her to heaven, but I heard her screams, and I can tell you: they came from hell. (*Beat.*) My poor dear sister. (*Beat.*) The child, of course, is my darling Freddy.

Grandchild of Kings
Harold Prince

Scene: Dublin
Serio-Comic
    Ella O'Casey: a young woman about to be married, 18-20

Here, Ella prepares herself for her wedding. A young woman madly in love, she can not stop thinking about the handsome young soldier—a drummer in the King's Liverpool Regiment – who she is about to marry.

O   O   O

ELLA: (*Drying herself and dressing.*) Everything would be stretchin' out in front of me fine if it wasn't for the mind of my mother. Think, now. Yes, everything is ready – the gold half-sovereign for the fee; though what a well off clergyman wants with a shining half-sovereign that I need so badly myself I can't guess and daren't argue about, for it is here and there and gone, like Hamlet's ghost; gone, but not forgotten, either, is the gold wedding ring that I'm minding, to be given to my love when I meet him at the front door of the church; the new dress, with its leg-of-mutton sleeves, carefully laid out over the back of a chair; the new frilled white petticoat carefully laid out over the dress; the snowy drawers, with deep flounces sweeping out around the edges, carefullly laid out over the petticoat; the garibaldi blouse prettily folded on the seat of the chair, and the pink stays nesting on the blouse; and my new high boots going half-way up the calves of my legs, and vivid blue bustle hanging by its ribbons from a hook in the wall – all well conserved for weeks in layers of lavender to entice and make glad the heart of the leading side-drummer in the first battalion of the King's Liverpool Regiment, best shot in the regiment, and regimental haircutter to the men.

Hand to Hand
Max Mayer

Scene: Here and now
Serio-Comic
    Terry: an auditioning actress, 20-30

Terry hasn't gotten a role in a while, so when the opportunity to read for a lead in a film comes along, she embellishes certain aspects of her past in order to get the part.

○   ○   ○

TERRY: I feel like a bit of a ghoul talking about this, but when you asked how I reacted to the character all I could think about was my sister. My sister, Thea, was six years older than me and I followed her around like a baby duck and tried to do everything that she did. Thea was thirteen that summer, but she was already sure she was going to be a great artist, a painter, and so I was going to be a great painter, too. My parents rented a summer house at the Cape and in the afternoons we'd go out to the beach and draw until just before the sun was going down and then Thea would show me her drawing and I'd marvel at how perfect it was. And I'd show her mine and she'd make a few haughty suggestions, but usually say something encouraging enough for me to repeat over and over to myself when I went to bed that night. Then, we'd run down to the water and have a last dip before heading home. I still have her drawing from that day. I had it framed, but I've never been able to put it up. When I look at it I can't believe we ever went in the water. There's a gray storm rolling in and there are three separate waves ripping in toward the beach. One breaking over the sand, one swelling up right behind the first one and another just a depression in the water halfway out to the horizon. Thea was already pretty good at perspective. Anyway, it was really a rough day, but that was okay because I had my inflatable plastic tube on, and the ones for the wrists that rolled on and held you up in the water while you were swimming.

And we were playing in and out of the waves and screaming when a big one would break over our heads and push us in toward the land. And then the undertow would drag us back out for the next one. And it all seemed fine because even though the water was up to my neck it was never really over Thea's waist even though we'd gotten quite far out to sea. My feet were still touching, but I just couldn't make any headway back toward the land and Thea couldn't either. And then we were out over our heads and the waves were still crashing and Thea was holding onto my tube and trying to ride the waves into the beach, but whenever she would catch one it would drive the two of us under and we would come up, choking and coughing on the salt water, even farther from the shore. And I started to scream at her to let go because when the waves hit us with her grabbing on like that I thought the tube was going to pop. And she must have thought the same thing because she hugged me really hard and before the next wave hit she let go of me and I never saw her again . . . So, I guess I can relate to your movie. There was one guy left on the shore by the time we went in swimming and he got in a pontoon rowboat and fished me out of the water, but Thea . . . drowned. And my parents sent me to a bunch of shrinks and stuff, but I don't think I started getting over it until two years ago when I went to this therapist who agreed with me that I'd killed my sister and that was just a fact of my life that I was going to have to live with. And somehow I was going to have to start forgiving myself for choosing me over her . . . No, it's okay. I guess maybe you could take it as a compliment. Your movie is a real story and I'd love to be part of it, if there's a place for me.

The House on Lake Desolation

Brian Christopher Williams

Scene: A hospital room, 1969
Dramatic
 Eloise: a patient in the hospital, 60-70

Eloise was brought to the hospital when her spine collapsed and has been comatose ever since. Here, she begins to come to, but clearly thinks that she is dead.

O   O   O

ELOISE: I used to be a dancer . . . but I imagine you already know that, don't you? You already know all about me.
(*Eloise begins to pirouette about the room.*)
[FRANKLIN: Eloise, do you know what year it is?]
ELOISE: Oh, I loved to dance. Any kind of dance. You know, I was a flapper. I bobbed my hair and exposed my knees and everything. Oh, there were no flies on me. Nothing compared to what these young girls are revealing nowadays, but oh I was really something.
[FRANKLIN: I'll bet you were.]
ELOISE: I have so many questions to ask you. The verses I've read are as clear as mud. How old was Elizabeth when you came to her? (*Beat.*) I thought so. I always believed she was over a hundred when she served you. They lived so long in those days. I'm just a spring chicken in comparison, aren't I? (*Beat.*) That's very kind of you to say. I like your outfit, but I did expect you to have wings. (*Beat.*) Oh, I see.
[(*Franklin is enthralled with her reverie.*)]
ELOISE: My baby, Gabriel, what special purpose do you have for him? Oh, I shouldn't ask that. Me not knowing is probably part of the master plan. But those other two, they met such awful deaths. Crucifixion and decapitation; oh, I don't think I could stand that. Couldn't my baby just die in his sleep. Does it have to be so Gothic. (*Beat.*) Perhaps you're right. Perhaps it's better not to know. I do have to think of the greater good. After all, this must

be some sort of an honor, to be chosen. Will I be made a saint? When they build my statues, Gabriel, I don't want to be wearing those robes you always see saints wearing. I want a nice print scarf and a hat, just like I wore when I went to the racetrack. I'll be our lady of the OTB. Yes, a big picture hat . . . but no heels. I'd hate to think of spending eternity in a pair of uncomfortable shoes. (*Beat.*) Well, I'm a practical woman. Maybe that's why he chose me. (*Beat.*) How exactly does this work? (*Beat.*) I mean the consummation; is it . . . do I get to enjoy it? I'm an old woman, Gabriel. It's been a long time. (*Beat.*) Oh, I'm a strong woman. I can handle the pain. They tried to give me morphine, but – what? (*Eloise turns to look. She goes over to inspect her I.V. drip.*)
When did they put that in? I thought I was flying solo. I hope they don't make me an addict. I wouldn't want my little baby to be born an addict. (*Beat.*) I see. Well, that's very reassuring. Thank you for telling me.
(*Eloise is again dancing about. She will dance over to the bed and get back under the covers.*)
Tell him I'm ready, Gabriel. I'm ready for my grand purpose. I always knew my life had a meaning. I'm a nurturer by nature. I truly am. Babies grow up, though. They grow up and push you away when you try to nurture. Mustn't overwater. You know, when I was a little girl, I was on pointe.

Hunters of the Soul

Marion Isaac McClinton

Scene: Here and now
Dramatic
   Hazel: an inner-city mother trying to cope with her dysfunctional family, 40s

Here, Hazel angrily confronts her son, who has turned to a life of petty thievery, and does her best to impress upon him the transitory nature of our lives.

O   O   O

HAZEL: You simply astound me sometimes. You know that? Always think that little weak ass game of yours gonna actually hurt somebody's feelings or save your foolish butt from itself. You more pitiful than a bottle of cheap wine sitting around waiting for some miracle to come along and change it to champagne. Shit . . . you don't even know if you wearing the game or the game is wearing you. You gonna need a brain surgeon to separate you from all of your bullshit.

[SYLVESTER: Why you gotta be cracking on me like that?]

HAZEL: Boy, in a hundred years, everything you see standing around you is gonna be gone. Long gone. Especially whatever you think that living is making for you. You can't keep it, Sylvester. And the more important things you lose you can't replace. What you lose in the world stays lost, boy. You don't never understand that.

[SYLVESTER: I understand what you saying to me.]

HAZEL: No you don't because you ain't never been smart enough to see things leaving you. Once it's gone, boy, it's gone. Impossible to put something else in it's place, to bring it back.

[SLYVESTER: I gotta drive.]

HAZEL: With all that money you making you gotta be scared up in your own house. Your mother has to deal with people pushing me out the way in my own home like I just clean up around here. You my savior, with all that money? You ain't saved me from nothing. Whether I take it or not, that money ain't gonna keep any kind of wolf from the door, in fact, it's gonna bring him howling and barking right up to the front door, foaming at the mouth, wanting to rip my throat out with its teeth. There is a tragedy coming down the pavement looking for you, boy. Got your name on a big list of fools. And it gonna get you. Grab a hold of you and choke your soul from out of your body. The thing that's the worst part is that a hundred years from now, hell, we ain't gotta wait that long, the next day, ain't a living soul gonna care. Not a single memory of who you were is gonna survive. You won't have left a mark, and nobody will even know you were ever here. You will be dead way before you die. You understand what I'm trying to tell you?

Hunters of the Soul
Marion Isaac McClinton

Scene: Here and now
Dramatic
    Hazel: an inner-city mother trying to cope with her dysfunctional family, 40s

Hazel's ex-husband, a man with whom she had a very complex relathionship, has just died. When Sylvester refuses to wear the tie that she has selected for him to wear to the funeral parlor, Hazel unleashes the full fury of her grief and rage.

O   O   O

HAZEL: DON'T YOU FOOL AROUND WITH ME TODAY, BOY!!! I'LL WALK YOUR ASS LIKE CHRIST WALKED THE WATERS!!!
[SYLVESTER: Come on, mother, chill. All this about some damn tie!]
HAZEL: YOU ARE GONNA WEAR THAT SOME DAMN TIE!!! YOU ARE GONNA WEAR IT OR I WILL HANG YOU UNTIL YOU ARE FUCKING DEAD, DEAD, DEAD, WITH IT!!! YOU UNDERSTAND WHAT I'M SAYING!!! YOU MIGHT NOT BE ABLE TO SHAM LOVING THAT MAN, YOU MIGHT NOT EVEN BE ABLE TO FAKE THAT YOU EVER GAVE ANY DAMN ABOUT HIM ONE WAY OR THE OTHER, I DO NOT CARE!!! IF HE WASN'T DEAD YOU MIGHT HAVE KILLED HIM WITH ALL THAT HATE YOU BEEN LIVING OFF OF OVER THE YEARS LIKE A VAMPIRE LIVES OFF OF BLOOD!!! BUT I DO NOT CARE!!! I DO NOT CARE WHAT YOUR TRUTH IS, I AM SICK OF HEARING ABOUT IT!!! ON THIS DAY, THIS NIGHT, YOU WILL LOVE THAT MAN'S TIE!!! I DO NOT CARE IF YOU CANNOT MUSTER UP ENOUGH LIES IN YOUR HEART TO CONVINCE HIS DEAD BODY THAT YOU LOVED THE MAN!!! THAT IS YOUR BRIDGE AND ALL THEM TROUBLED WATERS BELONG TO YOU!!! THAT IS YOUR SHIT AND FRANKLY I DO NOT CARE ABOUT YOUR SHIT THIS TIME!!! TONIGHT YOU ARE GOING TO SEE HIM, WHETHER HE IS ALIVE OR NOT, AND YOU ARE GONNA WEAR THAT MOTHERFUCKING TIE!!! YOU WILL DO THAT AT LEAST!!! NOBODY IN THIS WORLD GOTTA BETTER REASON TO HATE THAT MAN OUTSIDE OF ME AND I DON'T HATE HIM!!! I LOVED HIM!!! I

STILL DO!!! I UNDERSTOOD HIM!!! HE HAD TO GO WHEN HE HAD TO GO BUT I KNOW WHY ALL THAT CRAZY SHIT CAME DOWN!!! YOU DON'T KNOW A THING!!! HOW COULD YOU? YOU WERE A BOY!!! STILL ARE ONE IF YOU WANT MY OPINION!!! LIFE AND DEATH IS GROWN FOLKS SUBJECTS, YOU WOULDN'T KNOW ANYTHING ABOUT THAT!!! SO YOU JUST WEAR HIS TIE AND YOU LOOK ON HIM TONIGHT!!! YOU DON'T AND I WILL CUT YOU OUT OF MY LIFE LIKE A CORN ON MY FOOT!!! JUST LIKE NOTHING CAME OUT OF MY WOMB BUT A BUNCH OF DUST AND ASH!!!

John Dory
Craig Wright

Scene: The middle of the Pacific Ocean
Dramatic
    Mary: a young woman lost at sea, 20-30

Mary has been lost at sea for three long years and has recently lost her only companion. When a strange young man climbs aboard her little boat, she tells him the sad tale of how she came to be all alone at sea.

O   O   O

[JOHN: Mary –]
(*She covers her ears.*)
MARY: LA LA LA LA –
(*He tears her hands away from her ears.*)
[JOHN: Mary, I NEED you!]
MARY: SO WHAT, I NEED A LOT OF THINGS, I NEVER GET THEM, YOU'RE NOT SO GODDAMN SPECIAL.
[JOHN: I know that.]
MARY: We weren't put on this planet to be happy, you know. We were put here to BE here. (*Long pause. She pulls herself together.*) John . . . I ate my FAMILY. My MOTHER. She died first. We all . . . partook. My BROTHER, next. Then my FATHER. He had me . . . cut his throat right before he died . . . so I could drink his blood. It was awful. It was awful in a way that saying "It was awful" can NEVER communicate. It was like being torn open. Eating another person is like being torn open YOURSELF. And the only way I got through it was by believing that at the end of the nightmare, that there would be some life to go on to that would make sense of what I had done; what I had forced myself to do to survive. But that life never came. I never got rescued. I met some GUY . . . who made me a lot of promises and then broke them, left me for a mermaid WHO DOESN'T EVEN EXIST. And here I am.
[JOHN: With me.]
MARY: [Yeah, but so what,] one more pointless encounter with a

creep. Sorry, just guessing. But the POINT IS, when I die, like, later today . . . and I go wherever dead people go, I'll have to tell my mother and my brother and my father . . . "Sorry. I guess it turns out I survived for nothing . . . FOLKS . . . and . . . that you all died for nothing . . . FOLKS . . . and all that horribleness . . . and REAL HUMAN CHARITY, I mean, genuine moments of INVOLVEMENT . . . with HUMAN BEINGS . . . it was ALSO all for absolutely nothing, it was just a dream in our heads, it was just a big . . . fat . . . joke. But thanks anyway, really, maybe next time . . . oh yeah, I forgot, you only get one life."

[JOHN: Yeah, but so what?]

The Kentucky Cycle
Robert Schenkkan

Scene: A rude cabin in southeastern Kentucky, 1776
Dramatic
     Morning Star: a woman in labor, 16

Morning Star is a Cherokee who has been kidnapped from her tribe by the brutal Michael Rowen for the express purpose of providing him with an heir. As she suffers through the agony of childbirth, Morning Star calls in desperation to her lost people.

○   ○   ○

STAR: This child will kill me! Like the leaves in the time of changing colors, I am torn and scattered.
(*The Double screams.*)
Where are you, Grandmother?! You have turned your back on your people and we are no more. Cloudy Boy and even your Dog have abandoned us. The Four Witnesses hide their eyes and are mute. The Four Winds are still. All is death.
(*The Double screams.*)
It is the time of the Fall Bread Dance, and we gather to give thanks, Grandmother, for your bounty. The Great Game is close this year, but we women win and the men must gather the wood for the twelve days of feasting and dancing! Aaiiiieee! Laughing Eagle smiles at me, and my sisters whisper that his Mother will soon be talking to mine and bringing the gift of skins. Father frowns, but secretly I think he is pleased. Brother is chosen as one of the Twelve who will provide for the feast, and my heart swells so with pride it will burst! At dawn on the third morning, we gather to greet them at the Council House. See how he steps forward with the Grandfather of the Deer – horns like the branches of an oak tree!
(*The Double screams.*)
That night, my brother grows ill. Hot, like a fire, his skin burns to the touch. No amount of water can touch his thirst. He drinks streams and lakes. The Shaman dances, but he, too, is ill. We burn

now, all of us. Two days later, the blisters appear, stinging like red ants, like bees. I claw at my skin, my nails black with my own blood.

(*The Double screams.*)

The first to die are dressed and painted by their friends, as the great Grandmother taught us. Each is given a proper burial in the earth, but as more and more are dying, there is no one with the strength to carry his brother to the burial ground. My father dresses in his finest skins and feathers. He paints his face and sings his death song. He takes his shield and his lance and dares the Red Death to fight him in the Council House. The Red Death smiles at him and he dies.

(*The Double screams.*)

Everywhere is death. And I am the Noon-Day Sun who dreamed once, that she was a woman named Morning Star.

(*The Double screams.*)

Where are my sisters? Who will build my birthing hut? Where is my mother? Who will guide me through this time? Where are you, Grandmother! Why have you turned your face from your people? THIS CHILD WILL KILL ME!

(*The Double screams.*)

How I hated you, little one. When my blood stopped and my belly grew, how I hated you! You were part of *him*, my enemy, only now he was inside me. No longer could I shut him out, for there you were, always! How I hated you!

(*The Double screams.*)

But when I felt you move, child, when you whispered to me that you were *mine* – aaahhh, how then I laughed at my fears! *Mine!* You are *my* blood, and *my* flesh! We are *one* breath, and *one* heartbeat, and *one* thought, and that is DEATH TO HIM!

(*The Double screams.*)

Hurry, child – how I long to hold you!

(*The Double screams.*)

Hurry, child – my breasts ache for your touch!

(*The Double screams.*)

Hurry, child, and grow strong!

(*The Double screams one last time and collapses. Silence. Star*

raises an imaginary infant up to the audience.)
Michael Rowen, you have a son.
(*Michael turns. She looks at the baby and smiles.*)
He is born with teeth.

The Last Time We Saw Her

Jane Anderson

Scene: Here and now
Dramatic
> Fran: a woman who has just informed her conservative boss that she is gay, 40s

Fran's boss hasn't a clue as to why Fran wants everyone in the office to know that she's gay. Here, she does her best to explain it to him.

O   O   O

FRAN: I don't think you understand my situation, Mr. Hunter. I eat lunch alone every day because I'm terrified that people will ask about my personal life. I sit with a sandwich and a Cup O' Soup at my desk reading old copies of Computer News. People think I'm strange. I'm beginning to think I'm strange. I don't show up to office parties. I don't show up to picnics. I don't have drinks with our clients. When I go away for a conference, after the seminars I go straight to my room and order room service. I don't have a personality any more. I have nothing to bring home to Judith. We eat dinner in silence. The only conversation is directed to the cat. This is not my idea of a life.

Life Sentences
Richard Nelson

Scene: Here and now
Dramatic
    Mia: a young woman working in a garden, 20s

Here, a thoughtful young woman speaks of her love of gardening.

O   O   O

MIA: I love gardening. In my family, it's what one did when the world just got too complicated.
(*Beat.*)
We did a lot of gardening. Everywhere I lived, we had a beautiful garden. Flowers, vegetables . . . It's real. No bullshit. You sow what you plant; see what you grow; eat what you harvest. What could be simpler? My mother used to say that in her life that she'd spent a lot more "quality" time with vegetables than with men. (*She pulls out a weed.*) I used to garden with my mother. When I was a girl. It was a special time between us. No one else to complicate anything.
(*Beat.*)
Just us.
(*Beat.*)
I still hear her voice when I'm falling asleep. Still see her face – the face of my mother when I was a small kid. She'd even tell me bedtime stories that had a gardening theme and that always ended with the young sapling growing toward the sun – reaching for the sun. Or some variation of this. It was her effort to instill in me some sense of direction. Ever since I was a kid I have tried hard to be a sapling reaching for the sun.
(*Beat.*)
Whatever that means.
(*Beat.*)
My mother used to say gardening makes the world clearer. Just to

see a new bud, she'd say, makes sense out of so much else.
(*Beat.*)
When she dies, I'm going to make certain there are potted plants with fresh buds among the cut flowers, just as I have seen her do at a relative's funeral a few years ago.

Love Allways
Renée Taylor & Joseph Bologna

Scene: Here and now
Dramatic
Mother: a sad, empty woman, 30-40

Just before her daughter's Sweet 16 party, this woman takes a moment to offer the excited young girl some depressing advice.

O   O   O

MOTHER: I love it. And I love your enthusiasm. Stay that way. Always remember, it's no sin to be a woman. You were born that way; it wasn't your fault. This is embarrassing for me to talk about . . . I don't know whether you've noticed, or not, Gina, but your body's starting to change. When I was your age, I didn't notice because my mother wasn't as modern as I am; and I thought It was dirty to look at my body. Then when I was twenty-five, I was married and had two children already, so I was too busy to look. Now I'm forty-five and it's too depressing to look. Why should I make myself sick? Now that you're sixteen, you have a big decision to make – what kind of woman are you going to be? There are only two kinds – good and not-so-good. Let me tell you the difference. A not-so-good woman is only interested in pleasure and hot times and living only for the moment, and a good woman isn't interested in anything. It's live and let live. You don't bother me – I don't bother you. I left your father alone during the day and he left me alone at night. That was the joy of womanhood for me. My life had meaning. I was a good homemaker, a vivacious hostess, and a shrewd shopper. And in return, your father tried to be decent. Of course, things aren't always peaches and cream, but he never humiliated me in a large crowd. He never made me cry on my birthday. And he never ran off with a fan dancer behind my back. But when I had you, I was happy for one reason. I knew you would be part of a new generation of women; and these are my hopes for you. You can have what I didn't have. All the things girls of my generation could never hope to have – drive, ambition, talent, and self-respect. Today you can hold out for a man with all those qualities. Today you don't have to rush into marriage, because a woman can play football; she could lead a safari; she could climb a mountain. They're letting women in all the unions. So take advantage of it. You could be a bullfighter, a boxing referee, a stunt woman. Live dangerously! Try different things. Then after college, you'll become a teacher and get married. That's why you have children, so they'll have a little better life than you have. Oh, how I wish I had this talk with my mother when I was your age, today I might have had a real identity. I might have been Mrs. Somebody. (*Mother opens the door, revealing a foggily lit limbo area. Crying.*) Now, go downstairs to your party and grit your teeth and be a woman. It's all you have. Try to make it enough.

Love Allways
Renée Taylor & Joseph Bologna

Scene: Here and now
Serio-Comic
    Barbara: a new mother, 20-30

Here, an exhausted and ecstatic woman greets her child for the first time.

$\bigcirc$ $\bigcirc$ $\bigcirc$

BARBARA: You know, *you* really make me feel so glad I'm a woman. I can't imagine why I put you off for so long, but it's a big step our living together, when you consider we just met and I don't even know your name yet . . . What do you think of Ariella? It means lioness . . . Bad, huh? Okay. I won't push any name on you that you're not happy with. By the way, my name is Barbara, and you'll see I'm pretty progressive, as mother's go, although, I must insist that you always call me Mother because I'm the adult and you're the child (*Whispering.*) and I'm expecting you to love me. (*Pleading.*)
Please love me, I love you . . . Well, I don't really. Yet. But don't tell anyone. I don't want them to think I'm a bad mother. But I think it takes a little more time than three minutes, and I'm working on it. I do love you. I mean I don't feel *in* love. I don't know what I'm talking about. You're my first baby. I'm not sure *what* I'm supposed to feel . . . How's Eve? She was the first woman . . . Who cares, huh? I'll tell you something that'll probably surprise you. I'm scared about being a mother. Did you happen to hear anything I said while I was carrying you? I heard that infants are sensitive to their mother's feelings, so I forced myself to feel only good things about having you. I would really recommend natural childbirth to you, when you're ready and you're married. Not that I'm against a boy and girl living together if they're in love. Only, I would prefer if you didn't. How's Eunice? I don't know what it means. I only suggested it because it was your father's

grandmother's name . . . Okay, at least I can tell him I tried. How do you feel about having a working mother? Because I plan to go back to work in three months, and I'm telling you now I love my career and I'm not making any sacrifices because I'm entitled to have a life too. And you want the best of me, and you'll get the best of me if I work. We'll see. I'm open. And, I'm not giving up going out in the evening. We go out four, five times a week. Two, three anyway. And, I'm not giving up traveling. You'd better love flying . . . Robin, how's that? It means pretty bird . . . Eech! I'm exhausted. It's not easy being a mother. I hope you'll have patience. You like Patience? . . . Hope? Charity? Candy? Venus? Salome? Anne? . . . Anne's nice. Anna. A, my name is Anna. My mother's name is Barbara. We come from Cincinnati and we sell dictaphones . . . You know, you're silly. I love you. Anna? I think I'm *in* love with you, too.

Maybe I could get my leave of absence extended a few more months, anyway.

(*Barbara begins humming a free-form song, making up the words as she goes along.*)

Anna is a pretty little baby . . . And she's gong to love her mommy . . . And we're going to have such a nice time . . .

(*Lights slowly fade out, as Barbara improvises her little song to Anna.*)

Medea

Euripedes

Translated by Alistair Elliot

Scene: Corinth
Dramatic

Medea: A woman driven to murder by her husband's betrayal, 30s

Medea has sacrificed everything for Jason, who has now announced his intention to marry another woman and banish Medea. Driven by jealous rage, Medea here contemplates taking the life of their two young sons to punish Jason for his betrayal.

○　　　○　　　○

MEDEA: Oh children, children – so you have a city:
You'll have a home, to go and stay in always –
Away from your mother, leaving me to grieve.
For I am going somewhere else, to exile,
Before I get the joy of you and see
Your happiness, your weddings and your wives,
Before I decorate your marriage beds
Or hold the wedding torches over you.

What misery I have chosen for myself!
I suckled you, my children, but for nothing –
My labour went for nothing, all the scratches
Of fortune's claws, and crushing pangs of birth.
Such hope, I had such hopes of you:
That you would care for me when I was old;
When I died, your hands would wrap me for the grave –
The final wish of man. Those dreams were sweet
But they have come to nothing: bereft of you,
I shall drag out a life of pain and grief,
While you will never see your mother again
With those dear eyes, but change into another life.
My children, why are you staring at me so?
Why do you smile at me, that last of all your smiles?

What am I going to do? My heart gives way,
It betrays me, when I see their shining faces,
My babies. I cannot do it. Forget all the plans
I made before. I'll take my boys with me.
How can I harm them just to hurt their father,
When all his pain would be as nothing to mine?
I will not do it. [No. Goodbye, my plans.]

What's happening to me? Do I really want
To leave my enemies mocking me – and unpunished?
I must be brave, and do it. Coward woman,
To let soft arguments invade my heart . . .
Go, children; in; go in.
(*The Children start to go, but hesitate. She forgets them and
speaks the next line to the Chorus:*)

    And anyone
Who has no right to attend the sacrifices
Of this household, keep away:
My hand's not going to weaken.
No! No!
No, raging heart, don't drive yourself to this.
Not this! Not the children's lives: let them alone.
They'll live there with us – they will bring us joy.
No, by the vengeful spirits that live in Hades,
I shall not leave my children, I cannot leave them
To suffer the violence of my enemies.

It's all done now, in any case: there's no escape.
Surely the crown is on her head by now,
And in her golden veil the bride lies dying.
It's done.
    And now I take the road of dreadful misery,
And set my children on a worse road yet

Misha's Party
Richard Nelson and Alexander Gelman

Scene: The night of August 20, 1991. The Ukrain Hotel, Moscow. The Coup.
Dramatic
   Lydia: a woman engaged to an older man, 25

   Lydia is engaged to Mikhail, who is hosting a 60th birthday celebration for himself at the Ukrain Hotel. When she finds herself to be surrounded by Mikhail's bitter ex-wives, she describes her love for him in the following account of their first night together.

O   O   O

LYDIA: I don't feel like that anymore. I feel like tellin' everyone. Masha, you don't even know this, do you? (*No response.*) This man looks like such a practical, down-to-earth type of man, well, he has a very romantic streak in him, let me tell you.
[NATASHA AND KATIA: You don't have to tell—. (*They stop, realizing they are saying the same thing.*)]
LYDIA: (*To Masha.*) You went out one night. And he knocked—you didn't even know I was seeing your father at this time, I think. Or did you? (*No response.*) I guess she didn't. Perhaps if you had you would have been against it. But I'm sure once you could see how we felt about each other—we knew then you'd understand. Anyway, what was I talking about?
[MARY: When he proposed.]
LYDIA: We were in our apartment. Masha was out. We'd made love on the couch. He kept saying, 'What if my daughter comes back, let's go into the bedroom.' And I said, 'So what if she does?' And I held him, and in my hand I held—his weapon—.
[MIKHAIL: Lydia—.]
LYDIA: And what a weapon it is. I'm not embarrassed by this. And I said—experience, and I squeezed. And he put his hand between my legs and said—youth. And we both said—the perfect combination or something like that. And somehow or other, we started talking about living together, and then marriage came up, and he proposed. On your couch, Masha. That afternoon, I got a

little cold at one point and put that orange shawl you'd knitted, Masha, around both our naked bodies. In a funny way I felt that that shawl was like your blessing.

Misha's Party
Richard Nelson and Alexander Gelman

Scene: The night of August 20, 1991. The Ukrain Hotel, Moscow. The Coup.
Dramatic
    Katia: a woman sharing a painful memory, 40-50

Mikhail has invited all his ex-wives and their husbands to attend his 60th birthday
celebration. Here, his first wife, Katia, shares the sad story of his cruel dissertation of her.

O   O   O

KATIA: I remember—not laughing, but crying with Misha.
[FIODOR: Listen to this.]
KATIA: It was winter too. (*She eats, sips, continues.*) Perhaps the
same winter, Natasha. Masha, you were—five. And a beautiful
child. (*She takes another bite.*) I knew that Mikhail was seeing
another woman. We'd been married six years and this was not the
first. With some men—you know… (*Shrugs.*) It's the glands I
think. Then one afternoon, I was standing there at the kitchen
table and I can see him telling me: he's leaving us. Masha and me.
He's saying: Katia, I am leaving you. (*Beat.*) He's taking his things,
he's moving in with this woman, he wouldn't give me your name,
Natasha. Not yet. I try to joke with him—this is impossible. A wife
you can leave, but there's a child here, whom you love. (*She looks
at Masha, then takes another bite.*) But your mind is made up. It's
been an agonizing decision. This is why you've been so
preoccupied of late, you tell me. Because you'd been trying to
make up your mind. (*Beat.*) Suddenly I'm crying. I'm thinking crazy
thoughts—how are we going to live? I'm thinking: what are you
taking with you? I'm thinking: am I such a bad lover? I'd
wondered that often before—with the other girls he's gone out
with. The tears are pouring down my face and I'm hysterical. (*She
eats.*) He doesn't dare look at me, then Masha runs in—do you
remember this?
[MASHA: Yes.]
KATIA: She wants to know what is happening, so—I tell her. Your

father's running off with a whore. A bitch. This woman who is ruining both our lives. He tells me to stop it. Masha runs out of the room crying. She's screaming in the bedroom. I begin breaking things. You at first try to grab my arm but... (*Shrugs.*) Then I look at you, Misha. For the first time since you told me; and I see that you are crying too—weeping—uncontrollably. (*Turns to Natasha.*) Did he tell you this?

(*Natasha shakes her head.*)

I didn't think he would. This weeping—it calms me. I get control of myself. And I take Mikhail in my arms and say—it'll be fine. It'll be OK. And I kiss him on the cheek, on the forehead, on the mouth. I never loved you more than I did at that moment, when I was letting you go. (*Beat.*) That is why I never fought the divorce. I never hounded you for money. Two years you went without paying anything—

[MIKHAIL: I had nothing.]

KATIA: I said not one word. Because I loved you. Fiodor knows all of this. He's heard me tell this story a hundred times.

Moonlight
Harold Pinter

Scene: Here and now
Dramatic
    Maria: a woman remembering the past, 50s

Here, a woman about whom we know very little, shares happy memories from a more carefree time in her life.

O   O   O

MARIA: Do you remember me? I was your mother's best friend. You're both so tall. I remember you when you were little boys. And Bridget of course. I once took you all to the Zoo, with your father. We had tea. Do you remember? I used to come to tea, with your mother. We drank so much tea in those days! My three are all in terribly good form. Sarah's doing marvelously well and Lucien's thriving at the Consulate and as for Susannah, there's no stopping her. But don't you remember the word games we all used to play? Then we'd walk across the Common. That's where we met Ralph. He was refereeing a football match. He did it, oh I don't know, with such aplomb, such command. Your mother and I were so . . . impressed. He was always ahead of the game. He knew where the ball was going before it was kicked. Osmosis. I think that's the word. He's still as osmotic as anyone I've ever come across. Much more so, of course. Most people have no osmotic quality whatsoever. But of course in those days – I won't deny it – I had a great affection for your father. And so had your mother – for your father. Your father possessed little in the way of osmosis but nor did he hide his blushes under a barrel. I mean he wasn't a pretender, he didn't waste precious time. And how he danced. How he danced. One of the great waltzers. An elegance and grace long gone. A firmness and authority so seldom encountered. And he looked you directly in the eye. Unwavering. As he swirled you across the floor. A rare gift. But I was young in those days. So was your mother. Your mother was marvelously young and quickening every moment. I – I must say – particularly when I saw your mother being swirled across the floor by your father – felt buds breaking out all over the place. I thought I'd go mad.

Murmuring Judges
David Hare

Scene: London
Serio-Comic
    Sandra: a bright young policewoman, 20-30

Here, a policewoman on her way up the career ladder bemoans the endless amount of paperwork required to perform her job.

◯   ◯   ◯

SANDRA: You see, it's all mess. That's what it is, mostly. If you take the charge room for instance, there's maybe thirty or forty people arrested in a day. Most of them are people who can't cope. They've been arrested before – petty thieving, deception, stealing car radios, selling stolen credit cards in pubs. Or not even that. Disturbing the peace. Failing to appear on a summons. Failing to carry out conditions of bail. Failing to produce a current car license. Failing to fulfill Community Service. Getting drunk. Getting drunk and going for a joyride. Getting drunk and then driving home. Attacking your wife. Who then won't testify. Trying to cash a stolen cheque, only being so stupid you don't even try to make the signatures match. Opening telephone boxes. Fifty-fifty fights in clubs which are nobody's fault. Crimes of opportunity. Not being able to resist it. Then going back, thinking I got away with it last time. Possession. One acid tab. One Ninja Turtle sticker containing LSD. One smoke. One sniff. One toke. One three-quid packet. (*She smiles.*) That's the basic stuff. It's the stuff of policing. All you have to do with it is be a ledger clerk. You fill in bits of paper. Every officer carries thirty-six bits of paper about their persons at any one time.

My Left Breast

Susan Miller

Scene: Here and now
Dramatic
   Susan Miller: a woman battling the effects of breast cancer, 40s

When she drops her youngest son off at college, Susan is reminded of the panic that she felt on the day that she dropped him off at day camp for the first time.

O   O   O

SUSAN MILLER: He is twirling a strand of hair around his finger. We're in the Brandeis parking area, waiting to take our children to their dorms. It's an oppressive August day. Everyone has gotten out of his car, but Jeremy won't move. He's in the back seat, regretting his decision. There are no pretty girls. The guys are all losers. This was a big mistake.

Suddenly I'm in another August day. I've just put my eight year old on a bus to day camp. He looks out at me from the window. A pale reed, he is twirling his hair around his finger. I watch him do this until the bus pulls away. What have I done? I go home and fall onto my bed. I lie there and mourn all the lost Jeremys. My three year old, my infant boy. I lie on my bed and have grim notions. What if something happened to me and he came home from camp and I wasn't there to pick him up? What if I had an accident? Who would take care of him? What happens to the child of a single parent who is kidnapped by a madman? Then I imagine him lost. I see him twirling his hair as it grows dark in some abandoned warehouse. He walks the streets of a strange neighborhood. I know that he is crying in the woods. He has gotten himself into an old refrigerator. He falls into a well. He is in the danger zone. He has wandered too far from me. I have cancer and what if I never see him grown. "I'll go and get it back for you, Mom."

By the time I have to pick him up from camp, I'm frantic.

Somehow, we survived. Until now.

We get to his dorm and unload. His room is in the basement. It is moldy and I feel homesick. This isn't right. Parents move toward their cars dazed and fighting every urge to run back and save their young from this new danger – independence. (*Beat.*) When I get home, the sound of Jeremy not in his room is deafening.

One Man's Dance
Aaron Levy

Scene: Here and now
Serio-Comic
    Rebeka: a young woman getting ready to start college, 18

Rebeka has been in love with Ira ever since they were kids sneaking Margaritas when their parents weren't looking. Now, they both are facing the uncertain future that all college freshmen must face. On a last evening together before leaving for their respective schools, Ira complains that it won't be possible for him to follow his dream of becoming a filmmaker. In response, Rebeka shares a story that her father used to tell her when she was a little girl.

      O   O   O

REBEKA: *(Pause.)* My father used to tell me this Dot The Astronaut story.

[IRA: Dot?]

REBEKA: Dot.

[IRA: Dot.]

REBEKA: It's about this girl, who was always the same age as me no matter how old I got.

[IRA: Dot.]

REBEKA: She was born paralyzed – can't walk, can't reach out, can't dance. At night she and her father would sit on their balcony and look up at the stars, just like we are. One night, Dot asked her dad where Pluto was, that of all the stars she wanted to go to Pluto. Her father asked why Pluto? "'Cause I could dance on Pluto," she said. "I could dance with Mickey Mouse, and Goofy, and Donald Duck, and me."

(Beat.)

Her father pointed to the sky and said, all you gotta do is push those stars out of your way, and you can get there. That's all you gotta do. And if you get there, if you actually get there, Ira, it's not dark anymore. It's bright. "Then I can't get there," Dot said, "'cause I can't move, I can't reach." And Dot's dad held her up to the sky and said, "You can reach, if you just look up, get real mad at them stars, and push them out of your way. See? Look, there's Pluto, Dot. Don't be afraid, LOOK AT IT." (*Pause.*) And she looked, and her father raised her higher, and . . . he let go . . . (*Beat.*) And that's where she is, Ira – on Pluto, dancing with her pals.

Paddywack
Daniel Magee

Scene: London
Dramatic
    Annette: a young writer trying to break into journalism

Annette has just received a rejection letter from an editor. When her lover teases her about it, she unleashes the following torrent of anger and frustration.

ANNETTE: Colin, I'm not *trying* to break into journalism.

[COLIN: (*Can't resist a tease.*) Oh . . . silly old me . . . there I was thinking that submitting about ten articles a week sort of hinted that maybe you were . . .]

ANNETTE: For someone who thinks of himself as radical, you do come out with some startlingly true-blue perceptions.

[COLIN: Such as?]

ANNETTE: Your perception of journalism for one.

[COLIN: (*Amused at her annoyance.*) Oh, I see . . .]

ANNETTE: No. That's the point, Colin. You don't see. This positive little note from the editor which impressed you so much . . . this was the "pat" . . . you know, as in "pat-on-the-head" . . . as in "patronizing" . . . That little prick thinks I'm trying to break into journalism too.

[COLIN: Whereas?]

ANNETTE: I was *trying* to communicate a specific piece of information . . . namely, that the Irish Sea is being turned into nuclear soup . . . *that* is what I was attempting to do. *Not* break into bourgeois, bloody, so-called journalism . . .

[COLIN: OK, OK, . . . I'm sorry I . . .]

ANNETTE: And that's what I mean about your perception of it . . . The megalomaniacal little pricks who control journalism . . . seem to think news, people's lives, and what happens to them, is only there to give *them* something to do . . . Not the other, bloody way about.

[COLIN: OK, . . . I surrender, I'm sorry.]

ANNETTE: I wasted nearly two months digging up hard facts that point to the fact that if we don't get our collective finger out, we're all going to end up bloody glow-worms . . . And what's the reaction? "Have Patience" . . . (*Exasperated*) *God* . . . Next you'll be telling me that Russell Grant is a fucking journalist, *just* because he has a job on a newspaper.

A Perfect Ganesh
Terrence McNally

Scene: India, the present
Dramatic
    Margaret: a woman living in denial, 40-50

Margaret and Katherine have traveled to India, each on a separate quest of spiritual liberation. Margaret hopes to escape from the grim reality of the lump she has recently discovered in her breast. The Hindu god, Ganesha, has been monitoring their journey and has appeared to Margaret in the guise of a sympathetic Japanese tourist. Margaret finds herself teling Ganesha about the lump, and before she realizes what she's saying, she reveals a secret from her past that is darker and deeper than the lump.

MARGARET: Everyone thinks I'm a bossy bitch.

[GANESHA: It's a clever defense.]

MARGARET: I even fool Alan. Kitty's the one everyone loves. People like Kitty just have to be born to be loved. I've always had to work at it. I had my big chance and blew it. A son, my firstborn. His name was Gabriel. Such a beautiful name. Such a beautiful child. Gabriel. Never Gabe. Alan chose it. I used to love just saying it. Gabriel. Gabriel.

[GANESHA: What happened?]

MARGARET: [I don't want to tell you. Where's Kitty? I don't see Kitty.] We were in a park. Abingdon Square, Greenwich Village, in New York City. You wouldn't know it.

[GANESHA: Where Bleecker and Hudson and 8th Avenue all converge, just above Bank Street. Go on.]

MARGARET: I'd just bought him a Good Humor bar. Maybe you know them, too?

[GANESHA: Oh, yes; oh, yes! They're "sclumptious!"]

MARGARET: His little face was covered with chocolate. I took a handkerchief out of my purse and wetted it with my tongue to clean his face. He pulled away from me. "No!" I pulled him back. "Yes!" Our eyes met. He looked at me with such hate . . . no!

anger! . . . and pulled away again, this time hurting me. I rose to chase him but he was off the curb and into the street and under the wheels of a car before I could save him. Isn't that what mothers are supposed to do? Save their children. His head was crushed. He was dead when I picked him up. I knew. I wouldn't let anyone else hold him. They say I carried him all the way to the hospital a few blocks away. I don't remember.

[GANESHA: St. Vincent's. It's very famous. Dylan Thomas and Billie Holiday died there. I'm sorry.]

MARGARET: He was four years old. Gorgeous blond curls I kept long – you could then. I think he would have grown up to be a prince among men.

[GANESHA: All mothers do.]

[MARGARET: Do you have children?]

[GANESHA: No, and sometimes it is a great sadness to me. But only sometimes.]

MARGARET: I don't know why I told you this. Strangers in the night. Scooby-dooby-do.

[GANESHA: No, new friends in the Indian dawn.]

MARGARET: I've never told anyone about Gabriel. His brother and sister who came after. What would be the point? Alan and I never talk about it. This was years and years and years ago. We moved, we started a new family. I have another life. I wish I saw Kitty down there. The woman who drove the car was a black woman. We called them Negroes then. It wasn't her fault. She was devastated. I felt so sorry for her. During the service, Episcopalian, Alan's side of the family insisted, we're simple Methodist, we all heard a strange sound. Very faint at first. (*Ganesha has begun to hum the spiritual, "Swing Low, Sweet Chariot."*) We weren't sure what we were hearing or if we were hearing anything at all. I thought it was the organ but we hadn't asked for one. It was the Negro woman whose car had struck my son. She'd come to the funeral. I don't know how she heard about it. She was sitting by herself in a pew at the back. She was just humming but the sound was so rich, so full, no wonder I'd thought it was the organ. The minister tried to continue but eventually he stopped and we all just turned and listened to her. Her eyes were closed. Tears were

streaming down her cheeks. Such a vibrant, comforting sound it was! Her voice rose, higher and higher, loud now, magnificent, like a bright shining sword. And then the words came. (*She sings in a voice not at all like the one she has just described.*)
"Swing low, sweet chariot,
Comin' for to carry me home.
Swing low, sweet chariot,
Comin' for to carry me home."
(*Ganesha joins her.*)
"Swing low, sweet chariot,
Comin' for to carry me home.
Swing low, sweet chariot,
Comin' for to carry me home."

A Perfect Ganesh
Terrence McNally

Scene: India, the present
Dramatic
    Katherine: a woman on a spiritual quest for forgiveness, 40-50

Katherine shares Margaret's journey to India where she hopes to be able to escape the haunting visions of her son who was murdered in a gay-bashing incident. Here, Katherine confesses her humble origins to Margaret and tells the story of her courtship.

O   O   O

KATHERINE: I suppose George and I have a wonderful life but it's not what I'm talking about. I think these will make darling luncheon napkins. You know how I met him? I crashed a dance at the Westchester Country Club. My best friend and I, Flo Sullivan, we made ourselves fancy evening dresses and hiked our skirts up and carried our shoes and we walked across the wet grass on the golf course and snuck into the party through the terrace. The ballroom was so beautiful! Roses everywhere. Real ones. A mirror ball. Guy Lombardo was playing. Himself, no substitute but the real thing. This was a class affair, right down the line. Guy Lombardo and His Royal Canadians. "Begin the Beguine." I knew right away this was where I wanted to be and I would do everything I could to stay there. I would scratch, I would fight, I would bite. Barbara Stanwyck was my role model. George was in white tie and tails, if you can imagine him in such a thing. He had a silver cigarette case and was tapping one end of his cigarette against it to get the tobacco down. I thought it was the most elegant gesture I'd ever seen a man make. (*Lights up on Man. He is George, dressed in white tie and tails and tapping a cigarette against a silver case. He will dance to the music Katherine has described.*) We hit it off right away. I was a wonderful dancer. I'd made sure of that. I knew how to let the man think he was leading. With George I didn't have to. I knew he was going to ask me where I went to college. What I didn't know was what I was going to answer. When he did, it was during a Lindy. I closed my eyes, held my breath and jumped. "I graduated Port Chester High School and I'm working in the city as a dental assistant." "Great," he said. "I was afraid you were going to say you went to Vassar!" and laughed and lifted me up by the waist over his head for this incredibly long second, like we were two colored kids jitterbugging in Harlem and I felt a blaze of happiness, like I've never felt before or since! After two hours, I said, "Let me wear your class ring. For fun. We'll pretend." It was a Yale ring. I showed it to Flo in the ladies room during a band break. She couldn't believe it. She asked if she could try it on. I was washing my hands and it slipped out of my fingers and disappeared down the drain. What do you tell a man you just met two hours ago at a dance you crashed when you've lost his senior class ring? You don't tell him very much, Maggie. You sleep with him on the first date and you say "I do," after you make sure he asks you to bury him on the third. I mean, marry him. I can't believe I said that. Bury him.

Perpetual Care
Jocelyn Beard

Scene: Here and now
Dramatic
      An angel, 20-30

This angel has been sent to earth to observe the death of James Delacroix. In human guise, the angel has rented a room from James and has become quite friendly with him. When they share a cup of tea, James confesses his disappointment that his late wife never had an opportunity to know their grandchildren. Here, the angel does her best to provide him with some soul comfort.

O   O   O

ANGEL: (*Yes, different.*) What is a kiss, after all, but a gentle pressure here (*Lightly touches her lips.*) It's the love behind the kiss that makes it special, and Emma Mae's love cannot die. It lives in you and in every part of this house. It's in the purple paint and the creaky stair – third from the bottom – that she was always after you to fix. It's in the annuals that you plant year after year because that's what she did. It's in that worn spot in the floor in front of the sink where she spent so many hours standing . . . standing and talking to you as you sat right where you are now. It's everywhere, James, but best of all: it lives in the hearts of your grandchildren. Emma Mae didn't need to meet Davey and Tisha. She dreamed them as a young girl. She'd lie on her back in that big field of wildflowers behind her father's barn and imagine her life while clouds passed overhead. She dreamed all of you, and it was her amazing capacity for love that brought you all into being. She knew Davey and Tisha years before your old Ford broke down on County Road 44 and you had to ask the prettiest girl you'd ever seen if you could use her telephone. Do you remember, James? Do you remember what she said when you knocked at her door for the very first time?
[JAMES: (*As if in a dream.*) She said: "Well, it took you long enough."]

ANGEL: (*With a gentle smile.*) Yes. She'd been waiting for you, James. Waiting her whole life long.

Phantom Rep

Ben Alexander

Scene: The Eleventh Avenue Rep. Theatre

Serio-Comic

    Christie: an actress, 20-30

Christie has been locked in the theatre with Monica, a rival actress, who uses their forced time together to accuse Christie of using theatre as a place to assuage her vanity. Here, the spirited Christie sets her straight.

O   O   O

CHRISTIE: It was in the third grade, when they took us for a field trip to see *Richard III* in Boston. I'd never seen a live play before. I didn't understand what was going on up there, but I could tell that there was a whole bunch of people hating each other, going to war against each other, and just plain killing each other – kind of like all the wars and murders I heard about on the news. The last hour, I was really spacing out, desperately bored and upset with it all, wanting to go back to class and just take a spelling test or draw a picture. Then finally it ended and they closed the curtain. But then – right then – they did something that I wasn't ready for. They opened the curtain again, and there was everybody who'd been running around hating each other and killing each other for the last three and a half hours – they were all up there, holding hands, smiling at each other, patting each other on the back, smiling at us, taking a nice bow, and that was when it really hit me. Hit me hard. They looked so beautiful, so peaceful and loving. Richard the Third was standing right next to the woman he'd murdered, and she was holding his hand and smiling at him as if they were about to go get something to eat together as soon as they washed off their make-up and changed their clothes. And I had that picture in my head all the way back in the bus, and I lay awake in my bed practically all that night, thinking, that's what the world needs. We need to get the U.N. to pass a resolution that on a certain Sunday, everybody in the world – the

President of the United States, the head of Russia, the murderers, the bank robbers, the millionaires, the coal miners – will just line up and hold hands and take a bow. Dead people, too. I decided that dead people would suddenly be able to get up off the floor, walk over to the guy who killed them, and say, "Good show, good show. Ladies and gentlemen, we were only kidding. It was all a story. We really all love each other, and now we're going to change out of our costumes and have a party. You can all come too. Cake and cookies and wine, all on us!" And that's why I wanted to act: so I could do that. Whether I was playing Snow White or the stepmother, Cordelia or Lady Macbeth, I wanted people to see me get up off the floor and take my place in line, smiling and holding hands with everybody, so I could give them a taste of what it would be like if the whole fucking world could take a curtain call.

Pterodactyls
Nicky Silver

Scene: Here and now
Serio-Comic
    Emma: a hypochondriac with memory problems, 20-30

Emma's fiancé, Tommy, has fallen in love with her brother, Todd, who has AIDS. When Emma discovers that Tommy has contracted the virus from Todd, she shoots herself. Here, Emma's ghost speaks to us from the hereafter.

◯   ◯   ◯

EMMA: Hello everybody. I'm dead. How are you? I'm glad I killed myself. I'm not recommending it for others, mind you – no Dr. Kevorkian am I. But it's worked out for me. Looking back, I don't think I was ever supposed to have been born to begin with. Of course the idea that anything is "supposed to be," implies a master plan, and I don't believe in that kind of thing. When I say, I shouldn't have been born, I mean that my life was never all that pleasant. And there was no real reason for it. I was pretty. I had money. I was lucky enough to be born in a time and into a class where I had nothing but opportunities. I look around and there are crippled people and blind people and refugees and I can't believe I had the gall to whine about anything! I had my health – oh sure, I complained a lot, but really I was fine. And I had love! Granted the object of my affections was a latent, or not-so latent homosexual as it turned out, who was infected with the HIV virus, who in turn infected me and my unborn baby – but isn't that really picking nits? I can never thank Todd enough for giving me the gun, because for the first time, I'm happy. The pain is gone and I remember everything. Tommy is here, but we're not speaking. He spends all his time with Montgomery Clift and George Cukor talking about movies. I assume. And I've been reunited with Alice Paulker. We went to school together. She was shot last year by a disgruntled postal worker. She has long, wavy brown hair and skin so pale you can see right through it – I don't mean it's really transparent and you can see her guts and organs and everything. It's just pale. And she has very big eyes, green. And we listen to music and go for walks. We take turns reading aloud to each other. She reads poems by Emily Brontë and I read chapters from the *Tropic of Cancer,* by Henry Miller. She was always classier than me. And sometimes, we don't read. Sometimes, we just hold each other. And I run my fingers through her hair and she touches her lips, gently, along my cheek. She makes soft sounds, comforting sounds and she takes her time and runs her tongue along the edge of my ear. We take off our clothes and just look at each other. I was shy at first, but Alice helped me and never rushed me. She held my breasts in her hands and ran her lips between them, down my stomach. I touch her eyelids and her forehead and her hair and her fingers and the back of her neck. And she enters me and I am everywhere at once and nowhere at all. And I remember everything and find that nothing matters. And for a moment, for a moment or two that lasts forever, we become one person. And I forget, we forget, that we were ever alive. And everything makes perfect sense.

Slavs!
Tony Kushner

Scene: Moscow, March 1985
Serio-Comic
    Katherina Serafima Gleb: an inebriated young woman, 20s

Katherina is a night security guard at the Pan-Soviet Archives For The Study of Cerebro-Cephalognomical Historico-Biological Materialism. Here, she fantasizes about making her job a bit more glamorous.

KATHERINA SERAFIMA GLEB: (*Listens to the music a beat, then:*) Some nights I pretend that I am not simply night watchman but I lead midnight tours through here for insomniac Muscovites whose anxieties or guilty consciences keep them awake. This is my speech:
(*To audience.*)
Welcome to the Pan-Soviet Archives For The Study of Cerebro-Cephalognomical Historico-Biological Materialism, also known as PASOVACERCEPHHIBIMAT. Here the Party has stored the brains of its bygone leaders, an unbroken line of brains stretching back to Red October. Beginning of course with Lenin, most people think his brain is still in his body in the crypt, but it's not, it's here, it is MASSIVE, 1,340 grams of solid brainflesh, the heaviest brain ever extracted, it's a wonder the poor man could hold his head up his brain was so grotesquely HUGE. Ranked beside it are many other famous brains, all floating in some sort of sudsy lime-green mummifying juice, all the famous Bolshevik brains except for those which got flushed in the notorious dead-brain purges of 1937. Stalin's brain is here; Brezhnev's which is dingy-yellow like an old tooth; Andropov's, and now I suppose Chernenko's brain, which hasn't been delivered yet. Maybe they couldn't find it.
Let's talk politics.

Slavs!
Tony Kushner

Scene: Siberia, 1992
Dramatic
    Bonfila Bezhukhovona Bonch-Bruevich; a pediatric oncologist, 30s

As one who treats children's cancers, Bonfila is an unhappy witness to the devastating effects of exposing large portions of Russia's population to toxic materials of one kind or another. Here, she angrily confronts a government official.

BONFILA BEZHUKHOVNA BONCH-BRUEVICH: In Altograd, which is where I was before I was in Chelyabinsk, there's twenty times the normal rate of thyroid cancer. There's a lake full of blind fish. Everyone has nosebleeds. Everyone's chronically fatigued. Leukemia is epidemic. The reactor plant near there has cracks in the casing, steam comes through several times a month, it's the same kind as at Chernobyl, it was supposed to be closed, it isn't, and the caves in Chelyabinsk? The stuff you have in there, probably cesium, strontium certainly bomb-grade plutonium, piled up since when? 1950? It's seeping into the aquifer: sixty feet per year. Do you know what that means? There's a river nearby. Millions drink from it. This is documented. The Dnieper's already shot from Chernobyl, and people still drink from that. Millions. The plutonium in that cave. Three hundred pounds of it could kill every person on the planet. You have thirty tons down there, in rusting drums. The people of Altograd voted for you to move it, a referendum, last year: Why? Why hasn't it been moved?

Slavs!

Tony Kushner

Scene: Moscow, Siberia, 1992
Dramatic
 Mrs. Shastlivyi Domik: an unhappy angry woman, 40s

Mrs. Shastlivyi Domik's daughter has been deformed by her exposure to toxic materials. When she demands compensation for her plight from a government offical, he sidesteps the issue by trying to convert her to a new political movement. Here, the furious woman wastes no time in telling him exactly what she thinks of him.

○ ○ ○

Mrs. Shastlivyi Domik: (*Smiling.*) Listen, you fucking ferret, I'm not a fucking "Russian like you," I'm a Lithuanian, and I fucking hate Russians, and why am I here in Siberia, because fucking Stalin sent my grandma here fifty years ago. My grandpa and my great-uncles and great-aunts died tunneling through the Urals on chain-gangs. Their father and his brother were shot in Vilnius, their children were shot fighting Germans, my sister starved to death and my brother killed himself under fucking Brezhnev after fifteen years in a psychiatric hospital, I've tried twice to do the same – and my *daughter* . . . . Fuck this century. Fuck your leader. Fuck the state. Fuck all governments, fuck the motherland, fuck your mother, your father and you. –

Snowing at Delphi
Catherine Butterfield

Scene: Upstate New York
Dramatic
    Brenda: a woman 9 months pregnant, 20s

Brenda and her friend Allan have traveled to Nick and Sara's upstate home for Christmas. Sara is shocked to discover Brenda's pregnancy is the result of rape. When she asks Brenda if she's angry about her situation, she receives the following philosophical reply.

O   O   O

BRENDA: [Yeah, but so what else is new?] I've been angry since about 1972. It feels pretty normal to me. Did Allan ever tell you how we met?

[SARAH: No.]

BRENDA: They were wheeling me into Roosevelt Hospital. I'd tried to off myself, razor blades, you know? It was after the rape thing, I lost my job and they were evicting me, so I kinda thought razor blades was the best way out. But the landlord spoiled my plans and the next thing I knew I was in Roosevelt. Only once I was there they didn't know what to do with me, nobody knew me, no insurance, blah blah. They were going to send me someplace cross town, let me bleed over there. Just about that time Allan walks by. He was just visiting a friend and on his way out he sees what's going on. So he walks over and tells them he's my husband, can you believe that? That he just heard and rushed right over. So they admitted me, and the next day I woke up and there he was. He'd been there the whole time. When I asked him why he did it, he just said, "You needed help." That was it. "You needed help." I've been staying with him ever since. In my book, he's like a god. I know people think he's kind of weird and shit, but he's godlike to me.

The Stillborn Lover
Timothy Findley

Scene: A house on the Ottawa River, 1972
Dramatic
Diana: a woman who has just discovered that her father is gay, 20-30

Diana's father, Harry, has just been recalled from his post as Canadian Ambassador to Moscow following the mysterious death of a young Russian. When Diana finds out that the Russian was her father's male lover, she angrily confronts him with the lie of his life.

DIANA: Damn right I don't. Damn bloody right I don't. How can I? What am I supposed to understand? That all my life you've lied about who you are? That everything you said and did was a lie? (*Beat.*) God in heaven, father – I don't care *what* you are. But I have a right to know *who* you are – who my father *is.*

I cannot begin to describe how I have admired you all these years. How profoundly I have admired you. I looked upon you – I told that man in there – I told him that I looked upon you with wonder. *Wonder,* father, *God damn it.*

(*Almost loses control, but regains it.*)

It was always the thought of you, father, that saved me when other men battered me with their lies and self-deception. But I always knew they were lying. I always knew they deceived themselves about who they were and how righteous they were! They were bastards – every one of them! Every one of them *lied.* And they were so full of pride and self that most of the time they didn't even know they were lying.

Men are like that. Men are like that – but not you. Not you. You were whole. You were a whole man . . . true, above all other things, to yourself. I knew who you were. And now you want me to understand . . . I am given to understand . . . I am supposed to understand that I don't know you. All of a sudden – bam! An instant stranger. What am I going to do with this information, father? Not that you're queer – who gives a damn! But that you lied. You lied. You lied, like all the rest – and my problem is, I don't know where the lie begins – and I don't know where it ends.

The Stillborn Lover
Timothy Findley

Scene: A house on the Ottawa River, 1972
Dramatic
    Marian: Harry's wife, a woman in the early stages of Alzheimers disease, 50s

Marian's daughter, Diana, has just discovered that her father, an Ambassador in the Canadian diplomatic corps, is gay. Here, Marian confesses her strange role in Harry's covert life.

○   ○   ○

MARIAN: I keep thinking – there's something I must do. (*Pause.*) In Cairo . . . there was . . . (*Stops.*)
[DIANA: Mother? In Cairo? What.]
MARIAN: A young man. I . . . Something.
(*Music: Guitar. Step chords follow her through the following like a shadow.*)
Your father. In Cairo. The staff was made up entirely of men and boys . . . cooks, gardeners, drivers. The boys were messengers, mostly. Seventeen, eighteen years old, who lived all their lives in the streets. Desperate, all of them, for money. We used them as runners. Messages. Errands. There was . . . It was a time of crisis. A diplomatic crisis. Almost a war. There had been an assassination. The Americans had landed troops. The tension was palpable. Your father . . . (*Beat.*) There was a secretary. I can't remember his name. One of those blond men with eyes like blue ice. Efficient enough – but dangerous. He always wore a white linen suit – but there was something secretive about him – hidden. Then I found out what it was.
(*Marian, using the present, conjures the past. The garden becomes a courtyard in Cairo.*)
In the courtyard, there was a shed. This happened in the afternoon . . . The sun was blazing. I'd gone to the courtyard, thinking – I don't know – that I'd sit in the shade and read. But there was no shade. Then I remembered an umbrella – a sort of beach umbrella

– the kind you stick in the sand. And I thought – well, it's in the shed . . .

(*Marian re-enacts the way she went into the shed – opening the "door" with her arm. She removes her sunglasses.*)

The sun had blinded me. I couldn't see. I heard a noise – but I couldn't see what it was. And then I could.

(*Diana watches.*)

One of the messenger boys – a runner – was standing in the shadows. His back was to the wall. His eyes – I can still see his eyes. He was in some kind of ecstasy. And . . . the blond young man – the secretary – was kneeling in front of him . . . down on his knees in his white linen suit. I didn't understand, at first. And then I did. (*Puts the sunglasses back on.*) I turned and left them without a word. I don't really know if the secretary knew I was there. But the runner – he knew. His eyes had shown me that. And it was then – because I had seen his eyes – that I knew how I could save your father. Rescue him from the danger he was in. I could bring the runner to him. Offer him to your father. After all his years of silence and suffering, "Here," I could say, "is the answer to your pain, Harry."

[DIANA: And you *did* this?]

MARIAN: You don't understand, Diana. I was living with a man who was dying – of denial. Do you know what that does? It kills. And I had to save his life. *I* could not save it – not as me alone. Not any more. Not in that moment. Your father loves me, Diana. But I alone was *not* the answer to his pain.

Stones and Bones
Marion Isaac McClinton

Scene: Here and now
Dramatic
    Stony: a young black woman confronting her lover, 20 30

Bone has confessed to sleeping around with white women. Here, Stony asks him if their relationship would change if she were white.

○   ○   ○

STONY: If I could take my nose, and cut it, pull my flesh from off my bones and put on a skin made of peaches like it was a new winter coat, if I could look at you like you were a criminal all the time, cross to the other side of the street every time I see you coming my way, never wait on you first when it's your turn in line, never sit next to you on the bus even if it's the only seat, make you forget you had a mama that always looked old, and a daddy that always seemed broken, if I could make you forget the manhood that supposed to be in between your legs, make you dream in black and white, and turn the black to gray, if it were true that I had more fun, and knew what Clairol knows, and could make you feel it's all right and cool with me if you take every last bit of black that was passed down to you from every African hanging from your family tree, and trash it like it wasn't never there, wasn't never anything worth keeping no how. If I can get you to change how you talk, if I can refine all the loudness from out of your soul . . . if I didn't know nothing about nothing worth knowing about you . . . if I was white would I stop intimidating you so you could hold me through the night clutched to your chest? Would you be scared of me then? Would you stop being scared of yourself then?

Sunday on the Rocks
Theresa Rebeck

Scene: Here and now
Dramatic
    Jessica: a woman longing for marriage and children, 30

Jessica has been involved with commitment-shy Jeffrey for many years. Following a Sunday drive, Jessica returns home and tells one of her roommates that she thinks there's been a major breakthrough in Jeffrey's fear of matrimony.

O   O   O

JESSICA: This is one of the happiest days of my life. Why don't you believe me?

[GAYLE: I do. I'm sorry, I just – I'm so confused today. On the one hand, 30 seems young, on the other hand, 30 seems old. I think we should all be getting on with our lives, and I have no idea what that means anymore. So what did Jeffrey say?]

JESSICA: Well – it wasn't so much what he said. We were walking in the ocean, and the water was freezing; we were kind of laughing, about that . . . and there was this little girl running up ahead of us, chasing the waves in and out – you know, how kids do – and she had this giant piece of seaweed that she was swinging around, waving over the ocean. She looked like she was blessing the waters. So we started talking about kids, and how there were probably kids all over the world chasing waves, playing with seaweed – up and down the coast of Africa, and South America, and China and – the human connection felt so powerful. Thinking about all those people, all those children, on all those other shores. So we started talking about that, and – I don't know. He brought up – we started talking about getting married. I guess that sounds a little crazy.

[GAYLE: (*Dry.*) No. It sounds very romantic. Jeffrey's a very romantic guy.]

JESSICA: Then when we were driving home, we took all these back roads to avoid the traffic, and we ended up driving through what

93

must be the wealthiest suburbs in the country. You should see these places – Victorian estates, with manicured lawns and statues of little black men by the front gate – it was appalling. I kept thinking about how the earth is being destroyed, about how many beaches aren't safe anymore because everything's getting so polluted because American capitalists cannot see past their wallets or their lovely little lawns – And that's not even the worst of it. I mean, how do you think these grand American fortunes are made? They're built out of the ruined lives of South African blacks, or Brazilian peasants, or Korean factory workers. And you know, we're driving by these magnificent estates, and I just wanted to stop and say to these people: We are sharing this planet. All of us, we're all in this together. You have no right to be doing what you're doing. I wanted to tell them to go look at that ocean. Do you know what I mean?

Sunday on the Rocks

Theresa Rebeck

Scene: Here and now
Dramatic
    Elly: a woman in trouble, 30

Elly has just discovered that she is pregnant. Here, she passionately defends her decision to have an abortion to her pro-life roommate.

O   O   O

ELLY: I do! I want to do this! I don't want this baby to exist in the world. I don't care how awful that sounds; it's the truth. I'm tired of the way my life is just happening to me, all this stuff just keeps happening. My job, my boyfriend, my roommates, wicker furniture, Campbell's soup, a dead hamster; it's all beginning to blur together, and you think that some of this has got to be more important than the rest, but it gets to a point where you just can't make anything out. And I'm not saying that the world is a bad place to be; I'm not saying I wouldn't want a kid in the world. But my life is too blurred right now; it's like one of those bad dreams that just keeps going on and on and on and you just wish like hell that you'd wake up but it just keeps going; it's one cryptic, meaningless, confusing thing after another. But at some point, you have to say, hold it. Hold it. And I'm saying it now. A baby is not something that should just happen. This baby is not going to happen.

The Survivor: A Cambodian Odyssey

Jon Lipsky

Scene: The rice fields of Cambodia, 1970s
Dramatic
 Huoy My Chang: a pregnant woman struggling for survival in the Killing Field of Cambodia, 20s

Huoy is offered a bit of sugar by Pen Tip, a man who once turned her husband in to the Khmer Rouge. After an internal moral debate, Huoy gives in and eats the sugar. Here, she describes her delight in its sweet taste.

O   O   O

HUOY: Sugar. I love sugar. I love to suck on something sweet. I'm so sick in the mornings – sweets are the only thing I can keep down.

But I won't eat it right away. First I pray. For its soul, as if it had a soul, as if it were a living thing. I offer it up to Lord Buddha. Then I offer it up to my mother. And then I offer it up to my baby. And then I eat.

(*Eats the sugar.*)

It begins as a tingling on the tip of my tongue. Not a taste, but a tingling. That shivers the hairs on the back of my neck. Then the sweet shock washes over the sides of my mouth, and water floods up from under my cheeks. My heart begins to pound and I feel giddy, weak. Like something's tickling me. Something out of reach.

And . . . I swallow. Swallow it. A soothing flame penetrates my throat, opens my throat, spreads like a wound in my breast. Like a blood wound. Like a stain.

For a moment I feel like I'm dying but then this . . . this noise comes up from my belly, from my bowels and I have to breathe, have to catch my breath. I want to growl. I want to roar.

I hold my belly. Hold my baby. The walls of my womb quiver. Inside I think I feel my baby twitch and shake from all this sugar. I laugh. She laughs. We laugh and laugh, sucking on the sugar, me and my dancing baby.

The Treatment
Martin Crimp

Scene: NYC
Dramatic
  Anne: a woman trying to escape her abusive husband, 20s

Anne's husband keeps her tied up in their apartment. When she finally manages to escape, she decides to sell her story to a television agent. The agency is very interested in Anne's story and have put her up in an expensive hotel. Here, she speaks of her empty new existence.

ANNE: It's so hot in my hotel room I take endless showers. There's no bathroom *in* the room so I have to cross the corridor to the shower. The curtain is rotting especially at the bottom where it's permanently damp there's a kind of black mold growing on the blue plastic and people've left scraps of soap which I use to wash because I'm permanently scattered in this heat and I forget my own. So I take a shower with the scraps of soap then it's back to my room. I throw myself down on the bed and just lie there drying off in the current of air from the fan which I keep on maximum. For the first time in my life, my whole life, I'm completely free and alone and I can't bear it.
(*She drinks.*)
I've never traveled out of this *state* and yet I think I must be somehow jetlagged because I can't sleep but I can't really wake up – is that what it's like? I just go from the shower to the bed and back to the shower again and my thoughts are in a loop: how I replied to the ad never thinking anything would happen – then there was the call and the limo arrived – it was so *long* and white and cool inside and the driver never met my eyes – then you listened to my story and we went to the restaurant where I must've made such a fool of myself knowing nothing about anything, what to *order*, how to use *chopsticks, nothing,* what to *say* to you, and I reply to the ad and the call comes, and the limo

97

comes, and I tell my story, and we go to the restaurant and I just lie there staring at the fan which is like a person a disapproving person shaking its head going "no no no I don't believe this can be you Anne no no no no no no no . . . "

(*As she chants "no no no . . . " she moves her head slowly from side to side in the imitation of the fan, her eyes shut. Andrew comes behind her and gently takes hold of her head, stilling it.*)

[ANDREW: We could change your hotel.]

(*She opens her eyes. She moves away, sipping the drink.*)

ANNE: I've escaped from the man who silenced and humiliated me. So why does it feel like I'm betraying him?

Vladivostok Blues
Jocelyn Beard

Scene: an apartment in Vladivostok
Serio-Comic
    Sophia La Cruz: a Mexican soap opera star, 25

Sophia plays the title role in "Forever Angelina," a Mexican soap opera that is the number one show in Russia. During an arduous 10-city personal appearance tour that her manager insisted that she make, Sophia is kidnapped by a crazed fan in Vladivostok. When she realizes that her captor is relatively harmless, Sophia unleashes a passionate torrent of anti-Russian sentiment, none of which she actually means.

○   ○   ○

SOPHIA: Okay, Boris, let's get one thing straight: my name isn't Angelina. It's Sophia. Sophia Luisa Magdalena La Cruz, *entiende?* (*As if to a child.*) Angelina is the character I play on TV. She isn't real. She doesn't exist . . .

[PETYR: But . . .]

SOPHIA: . . . and if you dare to call me that name one more time, I swear to you that I will . . .

[PETYR: Shhhhh! Angelina, please! The Morales Gang may have followed us!]

SOPHIA: (*Staring incredulously.*) Morales Gang! That storyline is two years old, for chrissakes! (*Scornfully.*) Morales Gang. What kind of borscht-eating psycho are you, anyway? I told Stu that coming here was a big mistake. I mean, after all, it is Russia. But did he listen? Oh, no. (*Imitating Stu, her manager.*) "Do Russia, babe. It's your biggest market." Market my ass. I've been from one end of this shithole to another and all I've seen are lousy hotels with no toilet paper, undrinkable water, inedible food, bad booze (*Make ref. to Russian vodka.*), ugly buildings, and the people! My plastic surgeon could retire here! Oh, and the pollution! Before you say it, it's worse than Mexico City! Have you ever been to (*large industrial town with well-known pollution problems.*)? The water in my hotel was black, I tell you, black! And this is *my* market?

(*Imitating Stu again.*) "They'll treat you like royalty, babe. We'll live like the Czars!" Well, my gringo manager forgot one tiny little detail: you idiots had a revolution that wiped-out any remnants of civilization! You executed all the good-looking people, for chrissakes! And just look at what it's done to your gene pool! You placed the potato farmer and the factory worker at the top of your social ladder where the good-looking civilized people are supposed to be! It's no wonder that what few normal people are left are just dying to get out! Do you know how many resumés Stu has had shoved at him since we arrived? Thousands. That's right, thousands. Well, I say no gracias! When I get out of here I never want to see anyone or anything Russian ever again! I'm even going to talk to the network about pulling "Forever Angelina" from this market! Why a Mexican soap opera is the number one show in this mixed-up waste land is beyond me. It took my management two years – TWO YEARS – to get us a spot on American cable. Two years, and there are people in America who speak Spanish, let me tell you. Do you know that the woman who dubs my voice in Moscow weighs over three hundred pounds! And she has a disgusting wart (*Thrusting out her chin.*) right here! I tell you I will never make a personal appearance tour again! I shouldn't have to see three hundred pound women with warts dubbing over my love scenes! I'm a star, for chrissakes! I should be spared things like that!

Permissions Acknowledgments

ALCHEMY OF DESIRE/DEAD-MAN'S BLUES by Caridad Svich. Copyright © 1994, by Caridad Svich. All inquiries should be directed to John Santoianni, The Tantleff Office, 375 Greenwich Street, New York, NY 10013.

THE AUTOBIOGRAPHY OF AIKEN FICTION by Kate Moira Ryan. Copyright © 1991, by Kate Moira Ryan. Reprinted by permission of the author. All inquiries should be directed to Bruce Ostler, The Fifi Oscard Agency, 24 West 40th Street, New York, NY 10018.

BAILEY'S CAFE by Gloria Naylor. Copyright © 1994, by Gloria Naylor. Reprinted by permission of the author. All inquiries should be directed to Gloria Naylor, 638 2nd Street, Brooklyn, NY 11215.

BEFORE IT HITS HOME by Cheryl L. West. © Copyright 1993, by Cheryl L. West CAUTION: The reprinting of BEFORE IT HITS HOME by Cheryl L. West included in this volume is reprinted by permission of the author and Dramatists Play Service, Inc. The stage performance rights (other than first-class rights) are controlled exclusively by Dramatists Play Service, Inc., 440 Park Ave. South, New York, NY 10016. No professional or non-professional performance of the play (excluding first-class professional performance) may be given without obtaining in advance the written permission of Dramatists Play Service, Inc., and paying the requisite fee. Inquiries concerning all other rights should be addressed to Thomas Nye Swift, Attorney at Law, 614 West Monroe Street, Chicago, IL 60661.

BODY POLITIC by Steve Murray. Copyright © 1993, by Steve Murray. CAUTION: Professionals and amateurs are hereby warned that BODY POLITIC by Steve Murray is subject to a royalty. It is fully protected under the copyright laws of the United States of America, and of all the countries covered by the International Copyright Union (including the Dominion of Canada and the rest of the British Commonwealth), and of all countries covered by the Pan-American Copyright Convention, and of all countries with which the United States has reciprocal copyright relations. All rights, including professional, amateur, motion picture, recitation, lecturing, public reading, radio broadcasting, television, video or sound taping, all other forms of mechanical or electronic reproduction, such as information storage and retrieval systems and photocopying, and the rights of translation into foreign languages, are strictly reserved. Particular emphasis is laid upon the question of readings, permission for which must be secured from the author's agent in writing. Inquiries concerning all rights in the play should be addressed to Peter Hagan, Writers and Artists Agency, 19 West 44th Street, Suite 1000, New York, NY 10036.

CARELESS LOVE by Len Jenkin. Copyright © 1993, by Len Jenkin. Reprinted by permission of the author. All inquiries should be directed to the author's agent, Scott Hudson, Writers and Artists Agency, 19 West 44th Street, Suite 1000, New York, NY 10036.

THE CAVALCADERS by Billy Roche. Copyright © 1994, by Billy Roche. Published by Nick Hern Books. All inquiries should be directed to Nick Hern Books, 14 Larden Road, London W3 7ST ENGLAND. Available in USA from Theatre Communications Corp.

CONNIE AND SABRINA IN WAITING by Sandra Marie Vago. Copyright © 1989, 1994, by Sandra Marie Vago. ALL RIGHTS RESERVED. CAUTION: Professionals and amateurs are hereby warned that CONNIE AND SABRINA IN WAITING being fully protected under the copyright laws of the United States of America, the British Empire, including the Dominion of Canada, and all other countries of the Copyright Union, is subject to a royalty. All rights, including but not limited to, professional, amateur, motion picture, recitation, lecturing, public reading, radio, broadcasting, television, and the rights of translation into foreign languages, are strictly reserved. Particular emphasis is laid on the question of readings, permission for which must be secured from the author's agent in writing. All inquiries concerning the amateur performing and professional reading rights should be addressed to the Samuel French, Inc., 45 West 25th Street, New York, NY 10010-2751. All inquiries concerning all other rights should be addressed to the author's agent, Robert A Freedman Agency, Inc. at 1501 Broadway, Suite 2310, New York, NY 10036, without whose permission in writing no performance of the play may be made.

THE DARKER FACE OF THE EARTH a verse play by Rita Dove. Book publication by Story Line Press, Brownsville, Oregon, 1994. Copyright © 1994, by Rita Dove. Reprinted by permission of the author. All inquiries should be directed to Rita Dove, Dept. of English, University of Virginia, Charlottesville, VA 22903.

DESDEMONA by Paula Vogel. Copyright © 1994, by Paula Vogel. All rights reserved. CAUTION: Professionals and amateurs are hereby warned that DESDEMONA by Paula Vogel is subject to a royalty. It is fully protected under the copyright laws of the United States of America, and of all countries covered by the International Copyright Union (including the Dominion of Canada and the rest of the British Commonwealth), and of all countries covered by the Pan-American Copyright Convention and the Universal Copyright Convention, and of all countries with which the United States has reciprocal copyright relations. All rights, including professional, amateur, motion picture, recitation, lecturing, public reading, radio broadcasting, television, video or sound recording, all other forms of mechanical or electronic reproduction, such as information storage and retrieval systems and photocopying, and the rights of translation into foreign languages, are strictly reserved. Particular emphasis is laid upon the matter of readings, permission for which must be secured from the Author's agent in writing. Inquiries concerning rights should be addressed to William Morris Agency, Inc.; 1350 Avenue of the Americas'; New York, NY 10019; attn.: Peter Franklin.

THE ENDS OF THE EARTH by Morris Panych. Copyright © 1993, by Morris Panych. Reprinted with permission from Morris Panych, Talon Books, Ltd., Vancouver Canada. All inquiries should be directed to Patricia Ney, Christopher Banks & Associates, Inc., 6 Adelaide Street East, Suite 610, Toronto, Ontario M5C 1H6.

THE FAMILY OF MANN by Theresa Rebeck. Copyright © 1994, by Theresa Rebeck. All rights reserved. CAUTION: Professionals and amateurs are hereby warned that THE FAMILY OF MANN by Theresa Rebeck is subject to a royalty. It is fully protected under the copyright laws of the United States of America, and of all countries covered by the International Copyright Union (including the Dominion of Canada and the rest of the British Commonwealth), and of all countries covered by the Pan-American Copyright Convention and the Universal Copyright Convention, and of all countries with which the United States has reciprocal copyright relations. All rights, including professional, amateur, motion picture, recitation, lecturing, public reading, radio broadcasting, television, video or sound recording, all other forms of mechanical or electronic reproduction, such as information storage and retrieval systems and photocopying, and the rights of translation into foreign languages, are strictly reserved. Particular emphasis is laid upon the matter of readings, permission for which must be secured from the Author's agent in writing. Inquiries concerning rights should be addressed to William Morris Agency, Inc.; 1350 Avenue of the Americas'; New York, NY 10019; attn.: Peter Franklin.

FIVE WOMEN WEARING THE SAME DRESS by Alan Ball. Copyright © 1993, by Alan Ball CAUTION: The reprinting of FIVE WOMEN WEARING THE SAME DRESS by Alan Ball included in this volume is reprinted by permission of the author and Dramatists Play Service, Inc. The stage performance rights (other than first-class rights) are controlled exclusively by Dramatists Play Service, Inc., 440 Park Ave. South, New York, NY 10016. No professional or non-professional performance of the play (excluding first-class professional performance) may be given without obtaining in advance the written permission of Dramatists Play Service, Inc., and paying the requisite fee. Inquiries concerning all other rights should be directed to Peter Hagan, PO Box 30266, Port Authority Station, New York, NY 10011.

FLOATING RHODA AND THE GLUE MAN by Eve Ensler. Copyright © Feb 1993, by Eve Ensler. Reprinted by permission of the author. All inquiries should be directed to the author's agent, David Styne, Creative Artists Agency, 9830 Wilshire Blvd., Beverly Hills, CA 90212.

FLYIN' WEST by Pearl Cleage. Copyright © 1992, by Pearl Cleage. Reprinted by permission of the author. All inquiries should be directed to Howard Rosenstone, Howard Rosenstone & Wender, 3 East 48th Street, 4th Floor, New York, NY 10017.

GRACE by Doug Lucie. Copyright © 1994, by Doug Lucie. Published by Nick Hern Books. All inquiries should be directed to Nick Hern Books, 14 Larden Road, London W3 7ST.

GRANDCHILD OF KINGS by Harold Prince. Copyright © 1993, by Maestro Charley, Inc. and The Estate of Sean O'Casey. Reprinted by permission of the author. All rights apply to The Lantz Office, 888 Seventh Avenue, New York, NY 10106.

HAND TO HAND by Max Mayer. Copyright © 1994, by Max Mayer. All rights reserved. CAUTION: Professionals and amateurs are hereby warned that HAND TO HAND by Max Mayer is subject to a royalty. It is fully protected under the copyright laws of the United States of America, and of all countries covered by the International Copyright Union (including the Dominion of Canada and the rest of the British Commonwealth), and of all countries covered by the Pan-American Copyright Convention and the Universal Copyright Convention, and of all countries with which the United States has reciprocal copyright relations. All rights, including professional, amateur, motion picture, recitation, lecturing, public reading, radio broadcasting, television, video or sound recording, all other forms of mechanical or electronic reproduction, such as information storage and retrieval systems and photocopying, and the rights of translation into foreign languages, are strictly reserved. Particular emphasis is laid upon the matter of readings, permission for which must be secured from the Author's agent in writing. Inquiries concerning rights should be addressed to William Morris Agency, Inc., 1350 Avenue of the Americas'; New York, NY 10019; attn.: Mary Meagher.

THE HOUSE ON LAKE DESOLATION by Brian Christopher Williams. Copyright © 1994, by Brian Christopher Williams. Reprinted by permission of the author. All inquiries should be directed to the author at 10900 Bluffside Drive, #310, Studio City, CA 91604.

HUNTERS OF THE SOUL by Marion Isaac McClinton. Copyright © 1992, by Marion Isaac McClinton. Reprinted by permission of the author. All inquiries should be directed to the author's agent, Traci Weinstein, Don Buchwald & Associates, 10 East 44th Street, New York, NY 10036.

JOHN DORY by Craig Wright. Copyright © 1994, by Craig Wright. Reprint by permission of the author. All inquiries concerning production or other rights to JOHN DORY should be addressed in writing to the author's agent, Helen Merrill, Helen Merrill, Ltd., 435 West 23 Street, Suite 1A, New York, NY 10011, USA. No amateur or professional performance or reading of the play may be given without obtaining, in advance, the written permission of Helen Merrill, Ltd.

THE KENTUCKY CYCLE by Robert Schenkkan. Copyright © 1993, by Robert Schenkkan. Reprinted by permission of the author, care of the agent. All inquiries should be directed to the author's agent, William Carver, Writers & Artists Agency, 19 West 44th Street, Suite 1000, New York, NY 10036.

THE LAST TIME WE SAW HER by Jane Anderson. Copyright © 1994, by Jane Anderson. Reprinted by permission of the author. All inquiries should be directed to the author's agent, Martin Gage, The Gage Group, 9255 Sunset Blvd., #515, Los Angeles, CA 90069.

LIFE SENTENCES by Richard Nelson. Copyright © 1993, by Richard Nelson. CAUTION: Professionals and amateurs are hereby warned that LIFE SENTENCES, being fully protected under the copyright laws of the United States of America and all other countries of the Berne and Universal Copyright Conventions, is subject to a royalty. All rights including, but not limited to, professional, amateur, recording, motion picture, recitation, lecturing, public reading, radio and television broadcasting, and the rights of translation into foreign languages are expressly reserved. Particular emphasis is placed on the question of readings and all uses of the play by educational institutions, permission for which must be secured from the author's agent, Peter Franklin, William Morris Agency, 1350 Avenue of the Americas, New York, NY 10019.

LOVE ALLWAYS by Renée Taylor & Joseph Bologna. Copyright © 1993, by Renée Taylor & Joseph Bologna. CAUTION: Professionals and amateurs are hereby warned that LOVE ALLWAYS is subject to a royalty. It is fully protected under the copyright laws of the United States of America, the British Commonwealth, including Canada, and all other countries of the Copyright Union. All rights, including professional, amateur, motion pictures, recitation, lecturing, public reading, radio broadcasting, television, and the rights of translation into foreign languages are strictly reserved. The amateur live stage performance rights to LOVE ALLWAYS are controlled exclusively by Samuel French, Inc., and royalty arrangements and licenses must be secured well in advance of presentation. PLEASE NOTE that amateur royalty fees are set upon application in accordance with your producing circumstances. When applying for a royalty quotation and license please give us the number of performances intended, dates of production, your seating capacity and admission fee. Royalties are payable one week before the opening performance of the play to Samuel French Inc., 45 West 25th Street, New York, NY 10010-2751, or at 7623 Sunset Blvd., Hollywood, CA 90046-2795, or to Samuel French (Canada) Ltd., 80 Richmond Street East, Toronto, Ontario, Canada M5C 1P1. Royalty of the required amount must be paid whether the play is presented for charity or gain and whether or not admission is charged. Stock royalty quoted on application to Samuel French, Inc. For all other rights other than those stipulated above, apply to Bridget Aschenberg, c/o International Creative Management, 40 West 57th Street, New York, NY 10019.

MEDEA by Euripedes, translation by Alistair Elliot. Copyright © 1992, by Alistair Elliot. All inquiries should be directed to Oberon Books Limited, 521 Caledonian Road, Islington, London, N7 9RH ENGLAND.

MISHA'S PARTY by Richard Nelson and Alexander Gelman. Copyright © 1993, byRichard Nelson and Alexander Gelman. Originally published by Faber & Faber Ltd. Reprinted by permission of Faber & Faber Ltd. All inquiries should be directed to Faber & Faber, Ltd., 3 Queen Square, London WC1N 3AU, ENGLAND.

MOONLIGHT by Harold Pinter. Copyright © 1993 by Harold Pinter. Originally published by Faber & Faber Ltd. Reprinted by permission of Faber & Faber Ltd. and Grove/Atlantic, Inc. All inquiries should be directed to Faber & Faber, Ltd., 3 Queen Square, London WC1N 3AU, ENGLAND.

MURMURING JUDGES by David Hare. Copyright © 1991, 1993 by David Hare. Originally published by Faber & Faber Ltd. Reprinted by permission of Faber & Faber Ltd. All inquiries should be directed to Faber & Faber, Ltd., 3 Queen Square, London WC1N 3AU, ENGLAND.

MY LEFT BREAST by Susan Miller. Copyright © 1993, by Susan Miller. Reprinted by permission of the author. All inquiries should be directed to Joyce Ketay, The Joyce Ketay Agency, 1501 Broadway, Suite 1910, New York, NY 10036.

ONE MAN'S DANCE by Aaron Levy. Copyright © 23 September 1994. Reprinted by permission of the author. Inquiries should be directed to author at 2616 NE 113th St., Seattle, WA 98125.

PADDYWACK by Daniel Magee. Copyright © 1994, by Flamin' Eejits, Ltd. Reprinted by permission of Flamin' Eejits, Ltd. All inquiries should be directed to William Butler-Sloss, FLamin' Eejits, Ltd., 55 Greek Street, Soho, London W1V 5LR. Telephone (+44) 71 437 2900, facsimile (+44) 71 437 0930.

A PERFECT GANESH by Terrence McNally. Copyright © 1994, by Terrence McNally. All rights reserved. CAUTION: Professionals and amateurs are hereby warned that A PERFECT GANESH by Terrence McNally is subject to a royalty. It is fully protected under the copyright laws of the United States of America, and of all countries covered by the International Copyright Union (including the Dominion of Canada and the rest of the British Commonwealth), and of all countries covered by the Pan-American Copyright Convention and the Universal Copyright Convention, and of all countries with which the United States has reciprocal copyright relations. All rights, including professional, amateur, motion picture, recitation, lecturing, public reading, radio broadcasting, television, video or sound recording, all other forms of mechanical or electronic reproduction, such as information storage and retrieval systems and photocopying, and the rights of translation into foreign languages, are strictly reserved. Particular emphasis is laid upon the matter of readings, permission for which must be secured from the Author's agent in writing. Inquiries concerning rights should be addressed to William Morris Agency, Inc.,; 1350 Avenue of the Americas'; New York, NY 10019; attn.: Gilbert Parker.

PERPETUAL CARE by Jocelyn Beard. Copyright © 1994, by Jocelyn Beard. Reprinted by permission of the author. All inquiries should be addressed to Jocelyn Beard, RR 2, Box 151, Patterson, NY 12563.

PHANTOM REP by Ben Alexander. Copyright © 1994, by Ben Alexander. Reprinted by permission of the author. All inquiries should be directed to Ben Alexander, PO Box 377, Littleton, NH 03561.

PTERODACTYLS by Nicky Silver. Copyright © 1994 by Nicky Silver. CAUTION: The reprinting of PTERODACTYLS by Nicky Silver included in this volume is reprinted by permission of the author and Dramatists Play Service, Inc. The stage performance rights (Other than first-class rights) are controlled exclusively by Dramatists Play Service, Inc., 440 Park Ave. South, New York, NY 10016. No professional or non-professional performance of the play (excluding first-class professional performance) may be given without obtaining in advance the written permission of Dramatists Play Service, Inc., and paying the requisite fee.

SLAVS! by Tony Kushner. Copyright © 1994, by Tony Kushner. Reprinted by permission of the author. All inquiries should be directed to Joyce Ketay, The Joyce Ketay Agency, 1501 Broadway, Suite 1910, New York, NY 10036.

SNOWING AT DELPHI by Catherine Butterfield. © Copyright 1994, by Catherine Butterfield. CAUTION: The reprinting of SNOWING AT DELPHI by Catherine Butterfield included in this volume is reprinted by permission of the author and Dramatists Play Service, Inc. The stage performance rights (other than first-class rights) are controlled exclusively by Dramatists Play Service, Inc., 440 Park Ave. South, New York, NY 10016. No professional or non-professional performance of the play (excluding first-class professional performance) may be given without obtaining in advance the written permission of Dramatists Play Service, Inc., and paying the requisite fee.

THE STILLBORN LOVER by Timothy Findley. Copyright © 1993 by Timothy Findley. Reprinted by permission of Blizzard Publishing. All inquiries should be directed to Blizzard Publishing at 73 Furby St., Winnipeg, MB R3C 2A2 CANADA.

STONES AND BONES by Marion Isaac McClinton. Copyright © 1993, by Marion Isaac McClinton. Reprinted by permission of the author. All inquiries should be directed to Traci Weinstein, Don Buchwald Associates, 10 East 44th Street, New York, NY 10036.

SUNDAY ON THE ROCKS by Theresa Rebeck. Copyright © 1993. by Theresa Rebeck. All rights reserved. CAUTION: Professionals and amateurs are hereby warned that SUNDAY ON THE ROCKS by Theresa Rebeck is subject to a royalty. It is fully protected under the copyright laws of the United States of America, and of all countries covered by the International Copyright Union (including the Dominion of Canada and the rest of the British Commonwealth), and of all countries covered by the Pan-American Copyright Convention and the Universal Copyright Convention, and of all countries with which the United States has reciprocal copyright relations. All rights, including professional, amateur, motion picture, recitation, lecturing, public reading, radio broadcasting, television, video or sound recording, all other forms of mechanical or electronic reproduction, such as information storage and retrieval systems and photocopying, and the rights of translation into foreign languages, are strictly reserved. Particular emphasis is laid upon the matter of readings, permission for which must be secured from the Author's agent in writing. Inquiries concerning rights should be addressed to William Morris Agency, Inc.,; 1350 Avenue of the Americas'; New York, NY 10019; attn.: Peter Franklin.

THE SURVIVOR: A CAMBODIAN ODYSSEY by Jon Lipsky. Copyright © 1993, by Jon Lipsky. Reprinted by permission of the author. All inquiries should be directed to Bruce Ostler, The Fifi Oscard Agency, 24 West 40th Street, New York, NY 10018.

THE TREATMENT by Martin Crimp. Copyright © 1993, by Martin Crimp. Published by Nick Hern Books. All inquiries should be directed to Nick Hern Books, 14 Larden Road, London W3 7ST.

VLADIVOSTOK BLUES by Jocelyn Beard. Copyright © 1994, by Jocelyn Beard. Reprinted by permission of the author. All inquiries should be directed to Jocelyn Beard, RR 2, Box 151, Patterson, NY 12563.